# LEADERSHIP
# EMBODIMENT

Also by Wendy Palmer

*The Intuitive Body,*
*Discovering the Wisdom of Conscious Embodiment and Aikido*

and

*The Practice of Freedom,*
*Aikido Principles as a Spiritual Guide*

# Leadership Embodiment

*How the Way We Sit and Stand*
*Can Change the Way We Think and Speak*

**Wendy Palmer**

**Janet Crawford**

For information contact Emodiment International
http://embodimentinternational.com

PLEASE NOTE: The creators and publishers of this book are not and will not be responsible, in any way whatsoever, for any improper use made by anyone of the information contained in this book. All use of the aforementioned information must be made in accordance with what is permitted by law, and any damage liable to be caused as a result thereof will be the exclusive responsibility of the user. In addition, he or she must adhere strictly to the safety rules contained in the book, both in training and in actual implementation of the information presented herein. This book is intended for use in conjunction with ongoing lessons and personal training with an authorized expert. It is not a substitute for formal training. It is the sole responsibility of every person planning to train in the techniques described in this book to consult a licensed physician in order to obtain complete medical information on his or her personal ability and limitations. The instructions and advice printed in this book are not in any way intended as a substitute for medical, mental, or emotional counseling with a licensed physician or healthcare provider.

The Practice © 2013 Wendy Palmer
The Biology Behind It All © 2013 Janet Crawford

Cover Art: John Lund  http://www.johnlund.com

Photo of Wendy Palmer © 2012 John Lund
Photo of Janet Crawford © 2012 John Popplewell

Conceptual and Managing Editor: Joan Marie Passalacqua

Part One illustrations: 1a through 6a © 2013 J.F. Mahoney
http://www.candraw.net
Part Two illustrations: 8a, 9b, 10a © Janet Crawford; 8b, 9a © iStockphoto
Image editing by Richard Leeds

Book Design: Colleen Dwire  http://www.colleendwire.com

## First Edition / Fall 2013

Printed by CreateSpace, An Amazon.com Company

ISBN-10: 1492946699
ISBN-13: 978-1492946694
Library of Congress Cataloging Number: 2013949941

The Embodiment Foundation
813 Vendola Drive,
San Rafael, California 94903
email: office@embodimentinternational.com

*To our clients and students,*
whose inquiry, dedication, and growth
inspire us to continue our development.

– W.P. and J.C.

# CONTENTS

# EXERCISES

# ILLUSTRATIONS

# FOREWORD

## by Michael J. Gelb
### author of *How to Think Like Leonardo da Vinci*

This book is entitled *Leadership Embodiment.*
What is leadership? And what is embodiment?

Peter Drucker, the legendary management consultant, penned my favorite definition of leadership. He wrote, "Leadership is lifting a person's vision to high sights, the raising of a person's performance to a higher standard, the building of a personality beyond its normal limitations." The Free Online Dictionary defines "embodiment" as "something or someone that embodies a spirit or principle."

I first met Wendy Palmer 25 years ago on the aikido mat and have had the pleasure of attending her classes and teaching at her school over the years. I can confirm that she embodies the spirit and principles of leadership as defined by Drucker. In this very practical book, Wendy translates this spirit and these principles into a manual for elevating your vision, raising your performance, and expanding your character beyond normal limitations. This book effectively communicates the lessons Wendy shares in her aikido classes and her international workshops with you.

For example, Wendy writes, "Great leaders with a strong leadership presence can create the feeling of inclusion wherever they are—a meeting room, a big auditorium, a playing field, and even on a conference call. Everyone included in their expanded personal space has a felt-sense that they are part of something bigger than themselves." Now that's a powerful concept! This book is filled with similarly important notions, but what makes it especially useful is that each powerful idea that is presented is accompanied by a practical exercise for the reader to embody the insight. The exercises are accompanied by Jen Mahoney's vivid illustrations making it as easy as possible for you to learn and practice.

When I first bowed on to the mat at Wendy's dojo many years ago and saw a petite woman in the role of sensei, I was curious. Would she be able to effectively demonstrate Aikido techniques in response to real attacks from men who outweighed her by an average of about seventy-five pounds? As it turns out, yes, she could. But, what I liked most about Wendy's classes was her presence. She filled the dojo with it in a way that included everyone and gave us all a sense that we were part of something bigger than ourselves. She did this with an energy and demeanor that was intense, but poised; fierce, but not angry. Best of all, when Wendy had trouble unbalancing or throwing an attacker, she responded with grace and without egotism. Instead of trying to force or fake her technique, she demonstrated genuine curiosity, and in front of the class, she would attempt to work out how she could improve. She usually succeeded, but more important than the lesson in technique was the example of how to learn and how to teach without arrogance or narcissism. When Wendy writes, "the centered leader is brave and can welcome both success and failure with complete openness," it is not a theoretical construct, but again something she embodies.

One needn't be an Aikido practitioner to benefit from the lessons in this book. Aikido is a metaphor for resolving conflict in a creative and compassionate manner. This metaphor applies to our conflicts with others at home and at work, but most importantly, it's relevant to resolving our own inner conflicts. The ability to resolve internal conflicts in order to become more fully oneself is a critical key to developing as a leader. The exercises that Wendy has originated to help you accomplish this don't require any martial arts background or special equipment. They all begin with a simple but elusive need for us to "center" ourselves in the face of stressful circumstances. Centering manifests in a state of mindfulness that makes it possible for us to respond to challenging situations with creativity, consciousness, and compassion. When we are un-centered, we respond automatically from the less evolved parts of our brains.

The practical instruction provided in these pages is complemented with an exploration of the science that helps us understand how our physiology and psychology are related.

In the fascinating Part Two entitled *The Biology Behind It All*, Wendy's colleague, Janet Crawford, helps you understand how and why these practices work. Janet is a pioneer in the application of neuroscience to leadership, and after you read her incisive material your rational brain will be sold on the efficacy of the practices that you will learn from Wendy.

Beyond just validating the approach in Part One, *The Practice*, Janet aims to give you "a new lens through which to observe the human 'operating system'." She succeeds, and as you look through this new lens, you'll discover fresh strategies for managing the complexity of contemporary life, transforming stress into enthusiasm, and understanding yourself and others with greater accuracy and compassion.

# The Practice

**Wendy Palmer**

"In judging our progress as individuals,
we tend to concentrate on external factors
such as one's social position, influence and
popularity, wealth and the standard of education.

These are, of course, important in measuring
one's success in material matters and it is
perfectly understandable if many people exert
themselves mainly to achieve all these.

But internal factors may be even more crucial
in assessing one's development as a human being.

Honesty, sincerity, simplicity, humility, pure
generosity, absence of vanity, readiness to serve
others—qualities which are within easy reach
of every soul—are the foundation of one's spiritual life.

Development in matters of this nature is
inconceivable without serious introspection, without
knowing yourself, your weaknesses and mistakes."

Nelson Mandela, *Conversations With Myself*

# ONE

# Evolution of the Practice

Years ago, at the end of a workshop in Ireland, I received a defining compliment: "We have had many people come here and teach us about the 'what' of leadership. Wendy, you have taught us the 'how' of leadership."

This book is about the how of leadership. We will explore how our posture—the way we sit and stand—can change the way we think and speak. *Leadership Embodiment* (LE) practices develop centered, powerful leadership. Centered leadership incorporates mindful interest in the situation, the ability to shift from reactive reflexes to responsive choices, cultivation of a centered state of being, and the use of three energetic leadership competencies.

**1a-** Example of LE posture

Mindful interest means that there is openness to examining problems and the possible remedies while relating to a continual stream of discovery. This type of openness is the hallmark of a great leader and includes the practice of dropping the defensive mask of self-protection and allowing oneself to be transparent and accessible as a human being—one who wants to work with, rather than control others.

Acting and speaking from a responsive, centered state of being increases one's ability to see the big picture and be creative while being able to process more information and respond effectively.

The leadership competencies advanced by LE practices are: Inclusiveness, the ability to create an understanding and the felt-sense that everyone is in this together; Centered Listening, the capacity of being able to hear what is being said without taking it personally; and Speaking Up, the skill of speaking one's truth with clarity and precision while taking a stand.

During LE training, we explore our habitual reactions to stressful situations, then learn and practice LE techniques that shift the way we sit and stand to give us greater access to our innate capacity for wisdom, confidence, and compassion. LE training explores the realm of leadership with questions like: How do we tap the great potential that we all carry within us? What happens in those moments when we rise above our familiar responses to life's challenges and suddenly find insight, timing, and clarity flowing through us? LE techniques unify the content of what is being said with the non-verbal communication of posture.

## How Leadership Embodiment Evolved

For as long as I remember, I have been fascinated by how some of us are able to easily influence people and situations, while others struggle to get a response for their effort.

When I was young, I loved horses and had some wonderful experiences riding and training my own and my friends' horses. Through these experiences, I saw that non-verbal behavior affects interactions more than words. In school, I learned about great leaders who changed the world and I wondered how they were able to do it. Those leaders seemed to have an expansiveness that included entire nations as if a whole nation was their family. I wondered how they were doing that because I had to work so hard to sustain my connection with just three other family members.

I started paying attention to the posture and gestures of effective people and began to see patterns that were repeated in a variety of situations. I studied the non-verbal communication of countless people that included animal trainers, politicians, business leaders, military commanders, and spiritual leaders. I observed that those who were truly effective shared common ways of standing, sitting, and gesturing in relationship to themselves and others, especially in challenging and complex situations. These observations were enhanced through my study of the non-aggressive martial art of Aikido and my practice of mindfulness meditation.

As I simultaneously studied Aikido and mindfulness, I looked for the underlying principles governing an individual's ability to be effective in stressful situations.

## Aikido

The non-aggressive martial art of Aikido has always given me great metaphors for leadership. Aikido has shown me what a centered, powerful leader can accomplish in situations of conflict and overwhelming odds.

In Aikido we say that, "It is not the size of your biceps but the size of your spirit that makes the difference in how the conflict is resolved." When a leader is centered, their spirit expands their personal space to include their environment and everyone within it.

The study and practice of Aikido offer real in-the-moment opportunities for learning how to deal with stress and confusion. Aikido allowed me to learn how to fall skillfully—not just physically, but emotionally and psychologically as well.

Falling and then quickly standing up in a new position without stress or judgment is one of the gifts my body continues to receive from Aikido training. We call it "the art of falling." My whole being learned how to recover, adapt, and go forward within situations that are continually unfolding.

Many great leaders have said that they learn more from their failures than their successes and that their failures lead to success. This quote from Michael Jordan testifies to his relationship to failure, "I've missed more than 9000 shots in my career. I've lost almost 300 games. Twenty-six times, I've been trusted to take the game-winning shot and missed. I've failed over and over and over again in my life. And that is why I succeed." One of my favorite poets, Rainer Maria Rilke says, "The purpose of life is to be defeated by greater and greater things."

I believe that balanced, centered, and embodied leadership skills give us the ability to lead ourselves and others out of the dark morass of fear, our sense of scarcity, our deep-seated desire for security, and our need to fix things and into our full potential. The centered leader is brave and can welcome both success and failure with complete openness.

Powerful, centered leaders are adept at working with intensity without constricting. On the Aikido mat, this is shown in the ability to deftly manage physical impact. We learn how to deal with physical impact without collapsing or becoming aggressive. In Aikido, we speak of receiving the attack. We learn to relax and allow the resilience of our body and our personal space to act as shock absorbers.

My work to translate the concept and practice of skillfully receiving an attack into the psychological and emotional arena of leadership has been challenging. Nevertheless, it has yielded some of the most useful LE techniques.

On the mat, we learn by feeling the relaxed power of our

teachers. Then, little by little over years, we develop our ability to relax and be open while receiving impact. On the mat, we invite attacks so that we can practice, grow stronger, and develop capacity for tolerating the hit or grab with relaxation and openness.

In every day life, the impact we experience is not physical, but rather the impact comes in the form of words and thoughts. In LE trainings, we use partner and group interactions as we do on the Aikido mat to simulate stress. Rather than strikes and grabs, we use words, gestures, and mild physical pressure to simulate impact so that we can practice dealing with intensity and learn more skillful responses. During these exercises of simulated impact and stress, we examine posture, the way we use our muscles, and the quality of our attention. We work with LE techniques to practice relaxing and opening in the face of stress; we grow stronger as we develop our capacity for managing the negative connotations of words and thoughts.

## *Mindfulness*

Mindfulness is a wisdom tradition of individual practice in which one studies their thoughts and feelings as they occur. Practicing mindfulness helped me wake up and continues to keep me awake. As I became more aware of my habitual thought patterns and reactions, I noticed the bias of my thinking. As I acquired this knowledge, I began to be able to shift from reactive reflexes to responsive choices. As I sat in mindful meditation, I was removed from external stimulus and could notice that I was so caught up in judging and planning that I was not present in the moment. In my daily life, I began to notice the same thought patterns and then could choose to be present, more aware of my environment, and more interested in what people were saying.

I began to see my habits of judging, planning, and wanting things to be different than they were. I saw how these habits were coloring the way I experienced my interactions with the world. Before I began mindfulness practice, I thought that the world was coloring my thoughts and feelings. Now, I see that it is the other way around. With mindfulness, I am not at the mercy of what is happening to me because I can choose how I respond to events.

Learning and practicing LE gives us skills to be more effective leaders. We begin with taking a good look at our behaviors that arise when stress occurs. We use mindfulness to turn inward and become aware of our reactive thoughts that limit our choice of action. We come to realize how deeply the needs for control, approval, and safety are planted in our psyche. Mindfulness practice is not easy, but mindfulness opens the door for us to step into honesty and bravery.

LE training gives us tangible understanding and experience of how deeply we can resonate with our capacity for wisdom, compassion and confidence. We have tremendous resources available to us when we are in a centered state of being, able to include others, listen without taking what is said personally, and speak up for our truth. LE centering techniques and competencies rehabilitate our capacity for optimism.

## Biology and Neuroscience

To people accustomed to doing business in the Western world, the concepts presented in LE may initially seem foreign, bordering on new age. We live in a culture that privileges the rational mind, while tending to dismiss the somatic, emotional, and subconscious aspects of ourselves as irrelevant or counterproductive to intelligence. From a Western model, we feel we should have the mental fortitude to think our way out of stressful situations. Over the past several years, advances in biology and neuroscience have started to provide solid scientific evidence for why this is simply not possible.

A few years ago, I met Janet Crawford, whose company, Cascadance, specializes in helping leaders build organizations that leverage the best in human biology. A former environmental scientist, Janet has immersed herself in the study of recent advances in social neuroscience and evolutionary biology. We have had numerous rich conversations about the nexus between her work and mine. LE students are often fascinated by the biological underpinnings that provide probable explanations for the effectiveness of LE techniques. In that light, Janet has been my collaborator in developing this book and has provided the companion text which is the second part of this book, *The Biology Behind It All*.

Readers interested solely in learning the LE techniques can skip this biological exploration without affecting their ability to absorb LE concepts and use LE techniques. For those of you who want to know more about the science and research that supports LE practices, *The Biology Behind It All*, provides those components.

## *Growing Into Leadership Embodiment*

The state of centered, empowered, and embodied leadership is strengthened by repeated and ongoing practice, like a muscle that grows stronger through weight lifting repetitions. We can use the LE centered way of being to do the heavy lifting in all aspects of our lives—as formal leaders, and also as parents, friends, teachers, caretakers, family members, service providers, consultants…We can meet the weight of uncertainty and loss with ease because we are strong enough in our heart and our spirit to succeed, fail, adapt, and continue on with interest and enthusiasm.

The stories, techniques, concepts, and science in this book are presented with the intention of helping you understand how and why we respond skillfully or unskillfully, what we can do to live with more grace and wisdom, and how we can increase the amount of time we are in a centered state of being. You can use LE techniques at any time and any place to quickly shift from a reactive state to a more skillful and resourceful way of being.

The practice of LE gives us the gift of having a choice to be centered and mindful. When we are centered and mindful, we automatically act with wisdom, compassion, and power.

# TWO

# Language and Concepts

As we explore the cultivation and evolution of our human potential, we find terms and theories that shape the way we talk and think about our actions and the consequences of our behavior. The language we use and the concepts we employ create the context of our journey—pointing the way to deeper understanding.

The LE model includes distinct ways of describing and analyzing how we behave in stressful situations. Using LE techniques, we scrutinize our habitual behaviors, examine the way we sit and stand, and learn how to shift our state of being so we can give more skillful responses in our quest to unite mind, body, and spirit. This unity allows us to embrace life's challenges rather than trying to push them away. LE language and concepts form a container that enables us to move beyond theoretical understanding into the embodied experience of our centered leadership potential. LE techniques give us ways to access our creative abilities even in stressful circumstances. LE terms and concepts serve as tangible reminders of how to be strong, influential, full-potential leaders.

## Three Leadership Competencies

LE cultivates three leadership competencies that we define as creative abilities. Developing one's capacity to embody these competencies increases the creativity, clarity, and power that are essential for sustaining centered leadership, even in high intensity situations.

Great leaders have three competencies or creative abilities that make them effective:

1) Inclusiveness: the ability to use an expansive presence to send the non-verbal message, "we are all in this together;"

2) Centered Listening: the ability to listen for the whole and hear what is being said without taking it personally; and

3) Speaking Up: the ability to speak one's truth with clarity and precision—without aggression or collapse.

LE practitioners learn to establish a centered state of being and evoke the three LE competencies in order to be powerful, effective leaders. We have tremendous resources available to us when we are in a centered state that is open to being inclusive of others, enhances our capacity to truly listen, and enables us to speak our truth. As you read about these competencies in this book, you will find specific terms that I have developed to clarify communication and make the influence of non-verbal exchanges more comprehensible. Working effectively with people involves more than managing data. Effective leadership involves acknowledging that each of us transmits our moods and personal concerns throughout the environment in ways that influence process and outcome. Evoking and managing one's creative abilities are keys to powerful leadership.

### Stress Reaction and Personal Patterns

LE uses the term "personal pattern" to describe how we react to stress. Stress shows up in our bodies before it arrives in our conscious awareness. Most often, by the time we become aware of our stress reaction, we have lost our window of opportunity to make a choice about our behavior. LE techniques work directly and efficiently with the body's reaction to stress.

As you practice LE techniques, you will learn how to recognize your habitual stress patterns and then to shift to a skillful, centered way of responding. You will build your capacity for choice, the choice to respond creatively and resourcefully in stressful circumstances. Without a skillful means of responding, our reactions are at best, automatic inept habits, and at worst, disastrous fight, flight, and freeze behaviors. When we do not have an embodied awareness of the things that are preventing us from acting with confidence, compassion and wisdom, we will continue to be reactive which includes laminating nice behavior on top of our survival or stress reactions. It is never pretty when the laminate breaks and the reactivity rushes out. Becoming familiar with our personal patterns gives us the means to develop skillful ways of responding.

Even with years of training and practice, we are not likely to transform ourselves into people who no longer have stress patterns, nor would we want to. In some circumstances, our personal pattern or reaction could be crucial to our survival. We can, however, learn to recognize our stress patterns as they are beginning, quickly assess whether or not they are serving us, and then, when appropriate, give a knowing smile and shift to a responsive state of being that accesses the higher functioning of our brain. To be able to efficiently make this shift, we need to study ourselves, observe our stress patterns, and notice how they show up in the way we sit and stand. Through LE practice, we train alternative ways of responding—we must repeatedly practice centering with Inclusiveness, Centered Listening, and Speaking Up.

## *Simulators and Accelerated Learning*

Each of us has a unique personal pattern or fingerprint for how we handle stressors. What triggers a reactive pattern in one person may not trigger it in the next, at least not exactly the same way. The physical expression and shape of our pattern can be observed in our posture, the way we sit and stand. In LE trainings, we develop the felt-sense of our reactions and responses by noticing changes in our posture. LE techniques flush out our physical reaction patterns by using simulators for stress in the form of mild physical pressure, words, and thoughts. A stress simulator can trigger a reactive pattern in our bodies before we can even think of the story or have feelings about what is happening. Instead of asking, "What do I feel or think?" We ask, "What shape is my body taking?" Practicing with a simulator accelerates our ability to recognize our personal pattern as it emerges in our response to a particular stressor. We use LE techniques to acknowledge and become friendly with the reaction and then make the shift to our centered self which allows us to give a skillful response.

## *Personality and Center*

In order to further explore the differences between responding from center and reacting habitually, we make a distinction between two aspects of ourselves that, in the LE model, we call Personality and Center. This distinction helps us understand how we are sometimes capable of being wise, creative, compassionate, and courageous while at other times we become irritated, anxious, manipulative, and judgmental.

Personality is the part of us that strives to create safety in our lives. When we are operating from personality, our attention is focused on control, approval, and safety. People have asked if this is the same as the ego. Freud's definition of ego is a very complex term. Personality is like the part of ego that is bent on managing life so that it does not become chaotic. In LE terms, we say that the Head wants control, the Heart wants approval, and the Core wants safety.

**2a-** Examples of Personality Postures

When we are operating from Personality our focus is on safety and managing our environment. We want to be in control, have people like us, and feel safe. Given that life is not secure, unconsciously operating from Personality can be stressful in and of itself. Constantly attempting to manage every situation to achieve a desired outcome makes it very difficult to be skillful or creative, especially in threatening or stressful situations. Shifting to Center is a skillful way of neutralizing striving-for-control stress.

Center opens our perspective to interconnectedness and the big picture. When we are in a centered state of being, we know that we are part of the continuum of life that is creative, compassionate, and inquisitive. Center allows us to appreciate the fact that everything changes. When we are centered, we can open ourselves up to challenges, discover what is possible, and adapt. Center gives us access to: wisdom that comes from heightened perception and awareness; compassion from increased receptivity and openness; and confidence from the strength of vertical alignment. Center allows our natural responsiveness and creativity to emerge because we are not focused on safety. When we Center, our posture shifts. This shift in posture can influence how we think and how we talk about our thoughts.

**2b-** Examples of Center Postures

Our centered, uplifted posture physically changes our perspective and allows us to see more possibilities. An open, inclusive posture conveys a sense of interconnection that allows us to work together. The stability and strength of our uplifted posture allows us to embody and speak our truth without aggression or collapse.

As we train our attention to distinguish subtle shifts in body patterns and shapes, we are able to recognize the beginning of a reactive pattern and shift from Personality to Center. As we become more mindful of how we are focusing our attention, we become aware of how our attention opens or closes our access to possibility and choice. We ask: Where is my attention focused? Is my perspective narrow and limited in an attempt to manage the situation as in Personality? Is my perspective open and expansive, accessing probabilities and possibilities as in Center?

Given what we know about the deep survival patterns in our brain, the LE model does not expect to "transform" anyone into a person who is always centered and never reactive. We do, however, believe that you can increase your capacity to recover your balance and spend more time in a centered state of being.

## *Knowledge Is Not Enough*

We live in the information age where data and the exchange of ideas have been given precedence over our felt-sense experience and the biology that drives our physical existence. In an attempt to reconcile the difference between the ideas about communication and the biology that drives our behavior, books on self-development and behavior management abound. We are constantly being offered new theories on how to succeed while playing nice with others. If reading a book was all we had to do to achieve our full potential, then we would all be there. Part of the problem with just reading and understanding the information is that we do not have the embodied experience of the theory. When I read books on personal development, I am in a safe place, usually my bed or favorite chair, and all of the recommendations make sense to me. However, when I experience a stressful situation outside of my comfortable environment all those good ideas about how to work with stress go out the window.

Regardless of what I know, my system still becomes overloaded and I am suddenly reduced to a fight-or-flight-or-freeze survival pattern—in my case it is mostly fight. But, I have become my own best testimonial. Even though I still have the fight reaction, I have developed and learned to use LE techniques to quickly shift to more skillful ways of responding. I have embodied these LE techniques through ongoing study, training, and practice—you can too. LE techniques have made a tremendous difference in my life. My self-critic is at an all time low, and my confidence and enthusiasm are at an all time high. Practicing LE techniques guides us into embodying more satisfying and skillful ways to engage in interactions with ourselves and others. LE concepts and techniques are seeds to be planted in your awareness, but for them to grow and bear fruit, they must be cultivated by study, practice, patience, and repetition.

# THREE

# Inclusiveness

The message of Inclusiveness is: "We are in this together." Successful leaders know that people will work harder when they are inspired and feel included, but just knowing this does not make it happen. LE techniques give us ways to make it happen. When we are pressured and begin to tighten and constrict our bodies, we can use LE techniques to open and expand our presence and increase our capacity to be inclusive and inspiring. LE techniques are assets to support you in becoming a more inclusive and successful leader.

## *Leadership Presence*

Have you ever been in a place where you could feel someone's presence? Have you been near someone who was very happy or angry and felt his or her emotions radiating out into the room or environment?

Now, think of a great leader, someone who motivated and inspired you to action, someone who got your attention and earned your respect. Bring that person fully into your mind. What do you notice about their leadership presence? What are they communicating non-verbally with their posture, body language, and gestures? Most importantly, what effect are they having on the environment? Think about the way you feel when you enter their office, meeting room or any place where they are in a position of leadership.

A strong leader actually affects the environment around them without even saying anything. This is because they have an expansive leadership presence. They expand their personal space so that the environment and everything in it becomes an extension of them. These leaders have tapped into our brain's ability to automatically map in exquisite detail, the region surrounding our body. Neuroscientists have a special expression, "peripersonal space," to describe this region. In LE, we shorten the term peripersonal space to "personal space."

**3a-** Leader with expanded Personal Space that includes others

Sandra and Matthew Blakeslee describe personal space in *The Body Has a Mind of Its Own*. "Put your arms straight out in front of your body, as far as they can reach. Keep your hands flat, fingertips extended straight ahead. Now wave your arms up and down and sideways…This is the personal space around your body—what neuroscientists call peripersonal space—and every inch of it is mapped inside your brain. In other words, your brain contains cells that keep track of every-thing and anything that happens within the invisible space at arm's length around your body."

We also have the ability to map far beyond our personal space into what neuroscientists call "extra-personal space." In LE, we practice extending our personal space beyond our finger tips to include others and the environment and call the result "expanded personal space." Anyone inside a leader's ex-panded personal space can be mapped by the leader as part of themselves. A leader's stable, expanded personal space con-veys a felt-sense of leadership presence.

An effective leader's team does not consist of "other peo-ple." Rather, because of how our neurological system func-tions, a skillful leader includes their team as an extension of themselves. These leaders transmit the message, "We are in this together." Their presence affects you and everybody in the room without saying a word. These skillful leaders expand their personal space to include you and everyone around them.

## Expanding Personal Space Grows Leadership Presence

Strong leaders with strong personal presence can create a feel-ing of inclusion anywhere—meeting room, big auditorium, playing field, and even on a conference call. Everyone includ-ed in the leader's expanded personal space has a felt-sense that they are part of something bigger than themselves. This felt-sense of connection is an antidote to feelings of isolation and separation. Any group, be it family, audience, staff, or team, is unified when there is a sense of belonging and connection. LE techniques help you to better manage your personal space so you can affect your environment and those in it in a positive, non-verbal way.

The phenomenon of expanded personal space is described as being easily observed in elite athletes in *The Body Has a Mind of Its Own*: "When athletes are on the court or field, they are mapping the space around them and people in that space in ways that most of us cannot match. Their personal space and body maps, along with a newly discovered mapping system called grid cells, seem to be exquisitely developed, which may be one reason they score so many baskets and goals."

Expanding your personal space begins from the boundary that you notice when you first focus your attention on it. This boundary of your personal space is the starting place from which you can grow your leadership presence. Some people have asked, "How big can my space get?" My answer is, HUGE. Think of the Dalai Lama or the president of a large country when they speak in front of tens of thousands of people. I have been in a crowd with about twenty-five thousand people when the Dalai Lama was giving a talk. His leadership presence affected everyone in the space, having a positive effect on thousands of people at the same time. His strong and vivid presence is the result of a lifetime of spiritual practice that includes various forms of meditation and spiritual reflection for many hours every day. You may not be able to match the expansiveness of the Dalai Lama's leadership presence, but you can strengthen and increase your presence starting with what you have right now.

Our body heat can give us a sense of our personal space. Sensitive instruments can measure the heat radiating from your body. Think of a time when you or someone else had just completed some vigorous activity or exercise. You would be able to sense or feel the heat radiating from the energized body. You can use this sense of radiating heat to represent your personal space. Here's an exercise to help you develop your leadership presence.

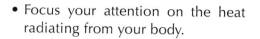

EXERCISE 1

# Developing a Felt-sense of Personal Space (PS)

**3b-** Felt-sense of PS

- Focus your attention on the heat radiating from your body.

- Imagine that this felt-sense of body heat represents your PS.

- Ask, "What is the size of my personal space?"

**3c-** Bubble of PS

- Think about your PS forming a bubble all around you.

- Add a color to the space inside the bubble that is your PS.

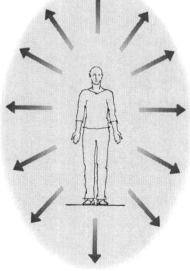

**3d-** Expanded PS

- Expand your PS to twice its size.

- Imagine that your PS has a cloud-like density that is different from the air in the room.

- Expand your PS even more.

- Ask: "How far can I extend my personal space?"
  "A few inches?"
  "A few feet?"
  "Am I able to fill the room?"

Here is a great way to practice growing your presence. Whenever you enter a room, look at the corners, assess the size of the space, and then extend your personal space to fill the room expanding it all the way into the corners. Use your intention to be inclusive so that the people in your expanded personal space feel they are a part of your vision and a part of a community. When you expand your personal space with Inclusiveness, everyone who enters the room will feel welcomed into your personal space. You will automatically be giving them the non-verbal message, "We are in this together."

Just like a muscle, your leadership presence and your capacity for Inclusiveness can be strengthened and developed. And as with your muscles, you are able to become more powerful through practice. Practice is repetition and training sustained over time. Daniel Coyle clearly states the importance of repetition in his book, *The Talent Code*. "There is, biologically speaking, no substitute for attentive repetition. Nothing you can do—talking, thinking, reading, imagining—is more effective in building skill than executing the action, firing the impulse down the nerve fiber, fixing errors, honing the circuit."

How much repetition are we talking about? There are differing statistics on the amount of repetition it takes to become accomplished in any skill. But a minimum of 500 practice repetitions seems to be required for gaining proficiency in any new skill. While the statistics vary tremendously, the bottom line is that you must focus your attention on consistently practicing the new skill over a sustained period of time, at least several weeks. The good news is that each repetition of expanding your personal space can take just five to twenty seconds so—depending on how many times a day you practice—you can get to 500 in a few weeks.

## Being Smart is Not Enough

Being a genius or having exceptional intellectual ability is not enough to coach a team or direct a company. Of course, being conventionally smart is important and useful, but managers who are exceptionally fast at processing information and data, can get so far ahead of their team that they create a state of disconnection and a sense of separation and isolation. When team members are disconnected, they do not work well with each other or their manager.

A cohesive team with collective intelligence is often superior to a single mind—even a brilliant one. The greater a leader's capacity for Inclusiveness, the more he or she can cultivate an atmosphere that inspires collective intelligence, creativity, innovation, and big-picture thinking. How does a leader influence the atmosphere? The first step is to learn how to expand your personal space and, as in *Exercise 1*, then to include others. When we extend our personal space out into the room including everyone there, we give the clear, non-verbal message and a felt-sense of, "We are in this together and we have the resources to meet this challenge."

Part of developing the capacity for Inclusiveness and leadership is studying what prevents us from being effective. We ask, "What prevents me from showing up as a leader?" "What keeps me from living up to my full potential? To answer these questions, one must become more mindful about the origins and manifestations of both skillful and unskillful behavior. With LE exercises and techniques, we explore our behavior and posture with simulations of the day-to-day stress of interacting and working with people. Then, we practice shifting from our unskillful reactive tendencies to skillful responsive postures and behaviors.

We use the LE postural distinctions of Personality and

Center as guides for making the shift from limited reactivity to inclusive responsiveness. When we react from Personality, we have a narrow focus that limits our options. When we shift to Center, we can respond skillfully from a broader, more inclusive perspective. When we get the hang of making the shift, we practice making the shift as opportunities arise throughout each day. The more mindful we are of Personality and Center, the more we can practice making the quick shift to Center, and the more adept we become. Each repetition of the shift strengthens our ability to be more skillful.

**3e-** Leader shifting from Personality posture to Center posture

## *Personality*

As a leader, you affect the people around you. On a good day when you are centered, clear, and confident things may go well and when stressful situations arise, you handle them with skill and grace. On the days when you are overwhelmed and acting from Personality, you may not be so skillful and revert to baseline survival reactions involving variations and combinations of fight, flight and freeze.

By fight we do not mean a physical altercation, but rather the tendency to express anger toward another person, stop the other person from talking, raising one's voice, and blaming others. For instance: An unexpected phone call in the morning puts me behind my normal departure time. There is more traffic that I expected and I realize that I'm definitely going to be late for my important meeting. I reach for my bag and spill tea on my shirt. As I get out of my car, someone talking on their cell phone bumps into me and in an angry voice I shout, "Watch where you're going!" Through the build up of stress, I became off center and my fight reaction was activated.

In an organizational context, flight is unlikely to show up as physically running away. Rather, in a group or interpersonal situation, flight is more likely to show up as disengagement behavior, including leaning back, looking away, ignoring what someone is saying, and "spacing out." Certainly someone is having a flight reaction when they leave a room before a discussion is complete but we can also leave the room mentally—we are not present when we are daydreaming about our upcoming vacation or thinking about what needs to be done when we get home.

The freeze reaction is the classic "deer in the headlights" phenomenon. During freeze, there is little physical movement and thought processes are suspended. We experience being stuck and unable to move or think about a course of action. Biologically, this serves to make ourselves invisible to a predator. In today's business environment, it is more likely to show up as your mind going blank just before a critical test or speech. Freeze is the experience that we all have had when we suddenly lose our ability to coherently say what we mean and sometimes turn into a blithering idiot.

Think of a time during a meeting when you felt tired, uncomfortable, or overwhelmed. When you became irritated or lost your center, did you have a fight reaction or a fight reaction or a freeze reaction?

When and how your fight, flight, and freeze patterns appear is determined by your Personality. These reactive patterns are developed in early childhood. Children unconsciously look for behaviors that will maximize their family members' acceptance and approval and minimize criticism and abuse. In addition, the young child's brain tends to encode and model survival behaviors from what they observe in those around them. Who better to mimic than their parents, who survived long enough to reproduce!

**3f-** Examples of contracted Personal Space in Personality Postures

Our Personality is the part of us that focuses on managing the stuff of life – people, things, and concepts. Personality is afraid of loss. Personality always looks for security. Every person has a particular pattern or way of organizing his or her body physically in an attempt to manage a situation to achieve maximum security and minimize any perceived threat. Under pressure or in stressful situations, people usually react from a Personality survival pattern that involves muscle contraction and a narrowing of perception. This somatic constriction triggers a shift from having a sense of connection and an inclusive perspective to a sense of individuation and a narrow focus. When you are in Personality, you are isolated and must manage the world around you.

These patterns show up in our bodies before they reach our conscious awareness. Small children and animals usually know before we do when we are mad, sad, glad, or afraid. Adults, on the other hand, are often divorced from direct access to what they are feeling, both emotionally and physically. As adults, by the time we realize that we are emotionally activated, we have probably been running that pattern for some time—minimally for seconds, but in some cases for hours or days. If you can learn to tune in to your body's patterns, you can recognize your stress reaction before it gains momentum. It is easier to shift from reaction to response when we are in the beginning stage of a personality reaction. In other words, when you first notice a reactive pattern beginning, you can offer your body the choice of an alternative responsive behavior. This alternative responsive behavior comes from an aspect of ourselves that we shall call Center.

## *Center*

Whereas Personality references on things, Center refers to unity and to the interconnection of all things within the expansiveness and fluidity of shared space. The centered state of being incorporates spaciousness in every situation, including the spaces between and around things. The centered state is naturally balanced, open, and inclusive. Remember Exercise 1 in which you practice changing the size of your personal space and leadership presence? Spaciousness is one of the keys to making the shift from Personality to Center.

Space unifies everything. Space is the largest component of an atom. Remember when you were in grammar school science class and you were taught that everything is made up of atoms? Images of atoms show that while an atom contains protons, neutrons and electrons, atoms are primarily made up of space. Outer space is so pervasive beyond galaxies, solar systems, and universes that, even with the most highly developed technology, there is no known end to space.

Space is the matrix of art. The utilization of space enhances objects, words, and notes. In music and poetry, it is the space between the sounds that creates the rhythm. In the visual arts of painting, sculpture, and photography, space is an element of design that enables the perception of images. The use of space can create a sense of calmness or a sense of stimulation. It is simply not true that things are solid and that space is empty.

In *The Silent Pulse* my dear friend George Leonard poetically describes a scientific view of matter:

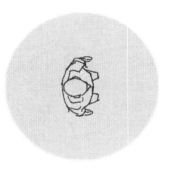

**3g-** Expanded Personal Space, top view

"The electron-scanning microscope, with the ability to magnify several thousand times, takes us down into a realm that has the look of the sea about it... As the magnification increases, the flesh begins to dissolve. Muscle fiber takes on a crystalline aspect. We can see that it is made of long spiral molecules in orderly array. And all of these molecules are swaying like wheat in the wind, connected with each other and held in place by invisible waves that pulse many trillions of times a second.

And what are the molecules made of? As we move closer, we can see atoms, the tiny shadowy balls dancing around their fixed locations in the molecules, sometimes changing position with their partners in perfect rhythms. And now we focus on one of the atoms: its interior is lightly veiled by a cloud of electrons. We come closer, increasing the magnification. The shell dissolves and we look on the inside to find... Nothing. Somewhere within that emptiness we know is a nucleus. We scan the space, and there it is: a tiny dot. At last, we have discovered something hard and solid, a reference point. But no! - as we move closer to the nucleus it, too, begins to dissolve. It too is nothing more than an oscillating field, waves of rhythm. Inside the nucleus are other organized fields: protons, neutrons, even smaller particles. Each of these, upon our approach, also dissolves into pure rhythm.

Of what is the world made? It is made of emptiness and rhythm. At the ultimate heart of the body, of the world, of the universe, there is no substance. There is only the dance."

Another key that helps to activate the centered state, is an uplifted and dignified posture. The act of sitting up and opening up has a positive effect on the chemistry of our brain. Our experience has shown that the uplifted posture of Center restores and cultivates our capacity for higher functioning: big-picture thinking, innovation, morality, and intuition.

Stress reactions mute our higher functioning capabilities and activate the short-term, survival-oriented reactions of narrow focus, hyper-vigilance, and defensiveness. The brain and the body are not separate—this living system we call "me" is an organic whole with every aspect resonating throughout all aspects of our mental and physical life.

In the LE centering practice, you learn to shift from your reactive contracted patterns into a more open, expansive, and inclusive states of being. LE training teaches you how to shift from constriction to expansion by using the extensor muscles of your arms and back. These extensor muscles uplift

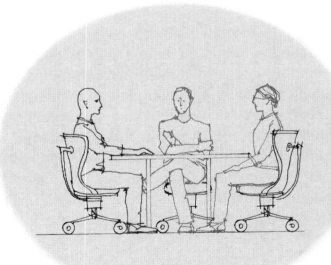

**3h-** With uplifted posture, the leader expands PS
to include others

your posture and extend your arms. This shift allows you to move from narrow focus to big picture thinking which gives you access to more resources for meeting the challenge of the moment. When you use LE techniques to shift to Center, you change your body's posture and the positioning of three major areas—Head, Heart, and Core. The uplifted posture and the vertical alignment of Head, Heart, and Core support you in responding more skillfully to internal and external stimulus. Your Head shifts from control to perception, your Heart from approval to compassion, and your Core from safety to confidence.

"Humans and other animals express power through open, expansive postures, and powerlessness through closed, constrictive postures. By simply changing one's physical posture, an individual prepares his or her mental and physiological systems to endure difficult and stressful situations, and perhaps to actually improve confidence and performance." From an article: *Power Posing: Brief Nonverbal Displays Affect Neuroendocrine Levels and Risk Tolerance*, Dana R. Carney, Amy J.C. Cuddy, and Andy J. Yap.

The LE centering process uses open, expansive posturing to cultivate confident, expansive performances. Centering exercises teach your body to shift from the constriction of Personality to the open expansiveness of Center. Understanding the need to shift with our mind is not enough. If understanding information were enough to change your behaviors then reading a book or manual about how you should behave would be all you need to live a balanced, happy, and productive life. Clearly that is not the case. Your body learns at a different pace than your mind, it needs more time and repetitions in order to get an "ah-ha" experience. Your body needs the experience of how to activate expansive, confident behavior, especially when you are under pressure and in stressful situations. In stressful situations, the body always wins. Even though you know better, once your system feels threatened, the reactive patterns of Personality will manifest. And so, we return to the importance of practice and repetition. In order to be skillful, we must repeatedly practice shifting from Personality to Center. Fortunately, life gives us many opportunities to practice everyday.

Because so many practice repetitions are needed in order to make the centered state a real option, it is important that the centering process be quick, easy, and appealing. The last thing you need is another chore on your "to do" list.

You can always shift from Personality to Center regardless of whether you are sitting or standing. The next exercise is an easy way to experience shifting to Center that you can practice throughout the day. Shifting to Center is a simple, quick way to focus your attention so you can shift from a tight, contracted, reaction state-of-being to an open, expanded, effective, and responsive way of being. This focus of attention and posture shift changes your chemistry in a way that allows you to have access to the creative, innovative, and inspired parts of your brain.

Even though this next exercise is described for a seated posture, you can also do it while standing, modifying details as appropriate. Take a few moments, right now, to try it.

EXERCISE 2

# Shifting to Center

**3i-** Personality Posture

**3j-** Center Posture

- Sit in a slightly slumped posture.

- Think of something you need to do but would rather not do.

- Let your mind go along with any resistance or irritation for about 10 seconds.

- Notice any sensations of constriction or negative thoughts.

*pause*

- Shift to an upright posture.

- Inhale and lengthen the back of your neck.

- Slowly exhale down to settle and relax your chest.

- Focus on your PS, expand it all around, above and below you with a sense of openness.

- Allow your shoulders to soften and settle with gravity.

*pause*

- Take a few moments to experience the felt-sense of Center.
- Think of the thing you would rather not do.
- Ask:

    Do I notice any difference in how I'm thinking about the task?
    Did my perception of it change?
    Did the task seem any less annoying or unpleasant?

If you answered yes, to any of the questions in Exercise 2, you had an experience of how changing your posture can change your perception. Your posture promoted the change of your mind. If just understanding something with your mind could change your perception and behavior, then you would be able to implement all of the preferred behaviors you have read about. In other words, you can not change your mind with your mind alone.

My point is that, just because you have read about a skillful ways to behave, even in this book, does not mean that you can activate that behavior when you are in stressful and overwhelming situations. You have to have deep, embodied experiences of the new way to behave in order to be skillful when you are under pressure. You get embodied experience by quickly practicing LE techniques throughout the day as stress arises.

## Using Simulators to Accelerate Learning

Flight simulators are used worldwide in the aerospace industry to train personnel. The simulators imitate the circumstances and create the physical conditions of emergency situations. These simulated circumstances allow crew members to experience and function in crisis situations before such crises arise on the job. When hazardous, sometimes life-and-death situations, arise in flight, the crew can function skillfully because they have repeatedly practiced how to respond. They have trained beyond theory and protocol, embodying skillful action and procedures.

Practicing preferred behaviors in stressful situations accelerates the body's learning. In LE trainings, we use stress simulators in the form of mild physical pressure, words, and thoughts so that we can become mindful of our reactive patterns. Stress simulators provide short cuts to more skillful behavior. When we are aware of our reactive patterns and recognize them as soon as they arise, we can use LE techniques to quickly shift to skillful ways of responding. Stress simulators hasten the process because they skip the emotional story you have about how you would like to respond. You might imagine that you will be relaxed, open, and creative in moments of stress and intensity, but that is not usually what happens. When we feel stressed or threatened, the primitive survival part of our brain does not opt for creativity—it opts for safety.

We do not use sophisticated equipment like flight simulators in LE trainings, although that would be great fun. Instead, we use mild physical pressure to simulate stress.

## Using a Stress Simulator to Discover Personal Patterns

Much of the LE in training involves partner exercises—each person takes several turns at being the leader. A key element of LE is to develop an awareness of what our posture reveals. Quickly recognizing your reactive postural patterns allows you to swiftly shift from reactive to responsive.

LE training partners create stress simulators for each other in order to trigger reactive postural patterns. When a personal pattern is provoked, we survey our posture and pay attention to three areas of the body, that in LE speak, we call: Head, Heart, and Core.

Your pattern is reflected in the position of these areas. **Head** reflects what is happening in your mind and the need for **control**. **Heart** represents your emotional condition and desire for **approval**. **Core** shows your ability to support yourself and impulse for **safety**.

The next exercise will stimulate your reactive patterns so you can get to know them.

EXERCISE 3

# Partner Front Push

**\*Safety tips to protect yourself and not be injured:**
1. Make sure that your partner holds your forearms slightly above your wrist joints so that the pressure and impact goes into the fore- arms and not into the wrist joint.
2. The pressure, while quick, should not be overly intense or jerky.

- Stand so you and your partner are facing each other.

- Extend your arms forward.

- Ask your partner to take hold of your forearms slightly above your wrists.\*

- Ask your partner to quickly apply a light pressure\* and sustain it. It is important that the initial application of the pressure be quick but not hard.

**3k-** Partner applies pressure

- Notice where and how your body constricts or puts up a bound- ary in an attempt to keep the pressure from entering into your personal space.
- Survey three areas of your body: 1) head and neck, 2) chest and arms, and 3) abdomen, hips, and legs.
- Notice the position of your Head, Heart, and Core.

**3I-** Examples of Personality Stress Postures:
Head forward, Heart forward, Core forward

To figure out your postural stress pattern, reflect on the position of your Head, Heart, and Core during the exercise and ask:

Did my head move forward or backwards or lock in place?

Did my chest move forward or backwards? Did my arms bend? If yes, how much?

Did my hips move forward, backwards or lock down?

Did my perception narrow and did I focus my attention on the person applying pressure?

What else am I noticing about the positions and sensations of my Head, Heart, and Core.

Your postural stress pattern is like a signature—unique to you yet similar in some ways to other people's stress patterns. Having a third person play the role of observer for this exercise can be helpful. The observer can give independent feedback about the patterns and shapes your body is taking.

Now that you have observed your reactive posturing by noticing the positions of your Head, Heart, and Core, you can use that information to gain insight into your personal stress reaction patterns. The positions that your Head, Heart, and Core take during the Partner Front Push represent how you behave in stressful situations. Use these sample questions to study your patterns:

- If your head comes forward: Do I like to take control?
- If the head moves back: Do I want more information?
- If you push out with your arms: Do I have a tendency to become emotionally defensive?
- If the arms draw in: Do I tend to suppress my emotions?
- If your hips move forward: Do I believe I can do the job?
- If the hips move back: Am I doubting that I can do the job?
- What other things does my posture tell me about myself?

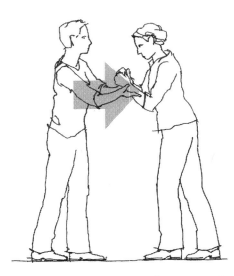

Each of us has a unique combination of control, approval, and safety postures and behaviors that are activated in pressure situations. Knowing and being aware of your Personality stress postures and behavior patterns is the foundation for being able to shift to Center and a responsive state-of-being.

Illustration 3m is an example of a stress reaction during the Partner Front Push exercise.

**3m-** Example of Personality postural reaction

The Head came forward and the gaze focused on the person doing the pushing. This person appears to want to control things with the mind and narrows the focus onto the source of the stress.

The Heart came forward but the arms bent and locked. This looks like the person wants a heart-felt connection, but is emotionally defensive or guarded.

The Core went backwards. This person may lack the confidence to get the job done.

In LE trainings, we repeatedly use a simulator exercises to practice centering while under stress so that we can embody Center during stressful situations in our day-to-day lives.

With these exercises, we cultivate strong somatic imprints of what it is like to be centered, uplifted, expansive, and relaxed while under pressure. During the next exercise, you will practice a way of physically exaggerating the expansion of your leadership presence. Exaggerating the expansion of your attention in this way gives your body clear direction for the shift you are making to expand your personal space to include both you and your partner.

The next exercise has three parts. First, you will flush up your personal reactive pattern; then, Center and use your posture to exaggerate the expansion of your personal space; and finish with dispersing increased pressure into your inclusive, expanded personal space.

Exaggerating the expansion of your personal space in this way gives your body a tangible experience of Inclusiveness. As in all LE partner exercises, valuable experience is gained when roles are switched. The stressor or person providing the pressure experiences a felt-sense of what it is like to be included or not, and how his or her ability to provide pressure changes when their partner shifts to Center.

EXERCISE 4

# Centering with a Stress Simulator

**\*Safety tips to protect yourself and not be injured:**
1. Make sure that your partner holds your forearms slightly above your wrist joints so that the pressure and impact goes into your forearms and not into the wrist joints.
2. The pressure, while quick, should not be overly intense or jerky.

## Part 1: Start the with the Partner Front Push exercise:

Ask your our partner take hold of your forearms just above your wrist.\*

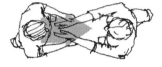

**3n-** Partner applies pressure, top view

Ask your partner to surprise you by applying light but quick\* pressure to your foreams and sustain it until you tell them to stop.

Notice how the same reactive pattern emerges again.

## Part 2: Change posture while under pressure from your partner:

- Inhale and uplift your posture.

- Exhale and settle into the earth.

- Look at a point to your **right**, far behind your partner, extend your fingers toward that point, and fully straighten your arm.

- Look at a point to your **left**, far behind your partner, extend your fingers toward that point, and fully straighten your arm.

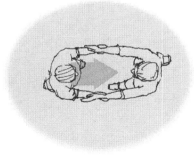

**3o-** Expanded PS under pressure, top view

- Keep your arms extended and expand your personal space.

## Part 3: Dispersing increased pressure and settling:

- Relax your shoulders and let your partner hold the weight of your arms.

- Imagine that the pressure from your partner is being diverted into your expanded personal space.

- See, feel, and sense the space between your two bodies and the space in the room.

- Ask your partner to slightly increase the pressure they are giving you.

- Consider that the pressure is being dispersed into the space around you.

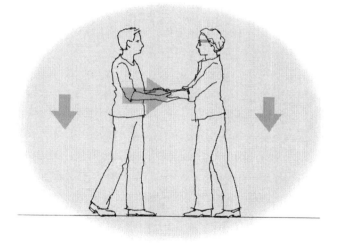

**3p-** Disperse pressure to PS and settle

- Imagine that your expanded personal space has become a shock absorber for the pressure.

- Allow yourself to settle with gravity into the accommodation of your expanded personal space.

Your body has just received the somatic imprint of what it is like to be centered, uplifted, expansive, and relaxed—all while under pressure. Using this exercise to simulate stress and then centering under pressure activates the "zone" or "flow-state" and gives you a felt-sense imprint of Center while under pressure.

Now that you have had an experience of what it is to be more centered under pressure you might think, "From now on, I will just center and suddenly I will have access to higher functioning aspects of the brain." Not so fast! It is important to realize that you must address homeostasis, the resistance to change.

Ecological, biological, and social systems are homeostatic in order to maintain stability. These systems oppose change with every means at their disposal. In his book, *Walking on the Edge of the World,* George Leonard beautifully describes why this is so. "...this homeostatic tendency, mediated by count-less feedback loops, deserves our praise before our blame, since it makes for stability and survival. But there are times when, in response to new challenges, systems need to change. At those times, it's essential that we at least understand that the built-in resistance is proportionate to the scope and speed of the change, not necessarily to whether it's ultimately adaptive or maladaptive."

Homeostasis is why even when you know you should be more open, kind, and relaxed, and stress occurs, you still con-strict and revert to your baseline personality pattern. Each of us reacts with our personal version of control, approval, and safety. The neural pathways for this pattern are deeper than the neural pathways for the centered response—so we easily revert to the pattern that is most familiar. This is why it is so dif-ficult to change the way we respond to stress.

The neural pathways for the centered response can be strengthened and deepened by ongoing repetition of the LE centering practice. Yes, it takes 300 to 500 repetitions just to get your foot in the door. So how are you going to manage to do all those repetitions? You can coach yourself to do them in five-second increments.

One client I was working with said, "I can't sustain the centered state." I responded, "You don't have to sustain it, just do it in 5 second bursts." "You mean like lizard pushups?" she asked. Yes, like lizard pushups—what a great image. If you have never seen a lizard doing pushups, you can Google "lizard pushups" to enjoy videos of them in action. You will see the lizard, as a display of strength, extend his front legs and uplift his body up to make himself look bigger and, expand his personal space, for just a few seconds. I really like reminding myself to do lizard pushups; they are quick, easy and – most importantly – they make me smile.

As you practice your ability to shift to Center, you can embellish each step—spending more time in each phase and deepening your felt-sense of them.

You can also abbreviate the LE Centering Practice so that you can use the technique quickly, on the run. The following two exercises are abbreviations of the LE Centering Practice. One is about twenty seconds long and the other is five seconds—both are reminiscent of lizard push-ups. These abbreviated versions make it easy to practice repeatedly throughout each day. Whenever you encounter intensity, be it the stress of failure or potential failure, or the exuberance of success or perceived success, you can quickly Center and be more skillfully present with the situation. You can get the number of your practice repetitions up and strengthen your ability to Center in a short time by using these abbreviated versions.

EXERCISE 5

# 20-Second Centering Practice

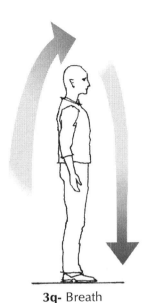

**3q-** Breath

1. **Focus on Breath** – Inhale up and out of the top of your head, lengthening your spine as you straighten and uplift your posture. Slowly take twice as long to exhale down your front all the way into the earth, softening your jaw and shoulders as you go.

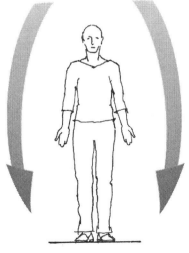

**3r-** Gravity

2. **Relate to Gravity** – Gravity is your natural way to relax. Feel the weight of your body and the weight of your arms pulling your shoulders away from your ears, and relax the tension in your jaw. Allow gravity to settle you into your personal space and onto the earth.

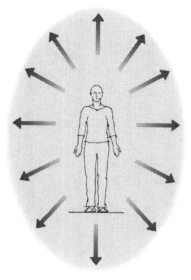

**3s-** Balance

**3. Balance Personal Space** – Ask yourself, "Is the back of my personal space, balanced and even with the front of my personal space? Is the left equal to the right? And is above equal to below? Expand your personal space out to fill the room.

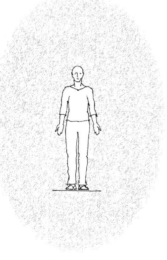

**3t-** Quality

**4. Evoke a Quality** – Your quality represents something you want to cultivate in yourself. Working with a quality is a practice of inquiry. Ask: "If there were a little more _____ (ease, confidence, compassion, etc.) in my body, what would that be like? If there were 5% more of that quality, what would that feel like? Where do I notice that quality in my body?"

# 5-Second Centering Practice

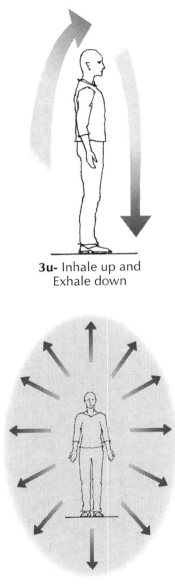

1. **Inhale** and uplift posture.

2. **Exhale** slowly and relax shoulders.

**3u-** Inhale up and Exhale down

3. **Expand** personal space to fill the room.

**3v-** Expand Personal Space

## Shaping Your Personal Space

We have talked about how one's personal presence relates to space around the body and how the size of the personal space is able to give a message of inclusion or exclusion.

Now, we will discuss how to work with the shape of your space. Consider the possibility of shaping and organizing space as a container for the message that you would like to communicate out into your environment.

In LE, we work with two basic shapes, circular or spherical, and triangular or wedge, in regards to our personal space. You must practice and develop your concentration in order to keep your awareness on the size and shape of the space you want to affect. Remember it takes more than just the notion of expansive leadership presence to really embody a strong presence that can hold the room. LE training uses the awareness of the shape of personal space to enhance leadership presence.

The shape of Inclusiveness is the circle or sphere. The circle is feminine, with a sense of embracing and inviting others in – receiving and accepting without the need to establish dominance or the desire to be appreciated. At the most basic level of life the circular egg invites and receives fertilization. As an archetype the circle implies collaboration and an urge toward unification.

**3w-** Circular Personal Space

The triangle or wedge shape is masculine. The point of a triangle can move efficiently through space and matter, as an arrow moves through air to penetrate a target and the bow of a boat cuts through water. At the most basic level of life, the triangular shape is represented by the pointed heads of sperm. As an archetype the triangle implies agency, assertion, and intense directed focus. In the chapter on Speaking Up, we will explore using the energetic triangular shape without aggression.

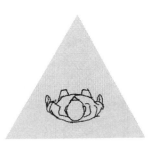

**3x-** Triangular Personal Space

## Cultivating Inclusiveness

The term "inclusive" is often used as an expression of willingness to embrace a diverse variety of people, projects, and possibilities. When organizations and companies declare themselves as inclusive," they mean that they are attentive to all the people involved in the work or project. This is the kind of inclusiveness that we advance and refine with LE techniques.

Like all creative abilities, the LE competency of Inclusiveness needs to be practiced in order to be attainable. Each day gives us many opportunities to strengthen our ability to be inclusive by consciously expanding our personal space. The more we practice expanding our personal space throughout the day, the more we are able to attain and sustain our ability to be inclusive.

Take a moment now to embody your brain's capacity to map your personal space by describing it with your arms. Extend your arms out and move them around—in front of you, to your sides, behind you and above you—use your arms to get a tangible sense of your personal space. Now, focus on enlarging your personal space. How much can you enlarge your personal space? How many people can you accommodate in your expanded personal space?

Based on your experience with the stress simulator exercises, remember what happens to the size of your personal space when you are stressed or threatened. Also, remember that you are now aware of LE techniques that you can use to center and expand your personal space so that you can be inclusive.

We all have had some experiences of being included and including others. The idea of inclusiveness is easily understood. However, the act of being genuinely inclusive can be challenging. Individuals may feel included in their family or not. When a family member withdraws or perhaps becomes isolated due to being shunned as the black sheep or elevated as the perfect one—he or she is no longer fully included the family space. The sense of group unity is lost. The same perceived lack of inclusiveness or unity can occur in work groups and teams of all sorts.

Generally a family, group, or team feels more cohesive and functions better when all members are included in the personal space of a parent, boss, or coach—everyone involved is supported by a strong leadership presence. Increasing the size your personal space develops your leadership presence. When people feel included and part of a collective, they become energized and inspired. The non-verbal message that "we are in this together" encourages everyone to contribute, to give a little more of themselves, and to collaborate because they are part of the collective. The optimal use of Inclusiveness is when each person expands their personal space to include others.

# FOUR

# Centered Listening

The second LE competency or creative ability is Centered Listening—listening for the whole, without taking it personally.

Every creature has ways of receiving information from their surroundings so that they can safely manage their interactions within their environment. Listening is an activity that involves receiving, processing, and interpreting stimuli. For human beings, Centered Listening is a multifaceted activity that includes what we hear, see, and sense. In LE trainings, we cultivate our ability for Centered Listening so that we can better understand and be more responsive to other people, the interactions of society, and the world around us.

As we develop our Centered Listening skills, we use the distinctions between Personality and Center to study our listening behavior. When we explore the different ways we listen, we find that our listening is influenced, and perhaps even hindered, by our motivations. Now, we will take a look at how Personality and Center effect what we see, hear, and sense.

## Listening from Personality versus Listening from Center

When we listen from Personality, we are driven by the need to bring about the desired outcomes of control, approval, and safety—most of what we hear during the interaction is filtered by these compulsions. Personality takes things personally, as if everything is happening to us rather than having the sense of participation in life.

When listening from Center, we are inspired by big picture, awareness of interconnection, and the abundance of possibilities—hearing and understanding the whole of what is being said. Center's perspective is expansive and inclusive.

A primary motivation for listening is data gathering—we want explanations and evidence that clarifies the material being discussed. An example is when we are actively listening to a lecture or a Power Point presentation on scientific data. When we listen from Personality, the desired outcome is to have more data so that we can manage the corresponding situation and prove our mastery which gives us a sense of control, approval, and safety. When we listen from Center, we can expand our perspective to cultivate big-picture thinking, open to more choice, and be skillful in our decisions.

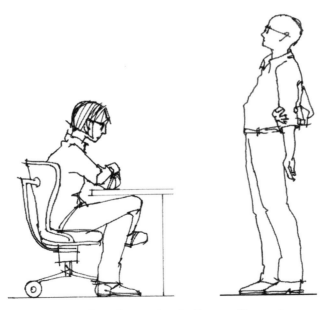

**4a-** Examples of Listening in Personality posture

Another motivation for listening is to make a connection that makes the speaker feel heard and accepted. In this case, the data becomes secondary to generating a feeling of connection. There are a several listening techniques that teach people to listen from the reference point of connection. Active Listening is probably the most well known of these techniques. Active Listening requires the listener to give feedback to the speaker by restating or paraphrasing what he or she has heard in his or her own words. The purpose of Active Listening can be to confirm that both parties are on the same page and to make a connection with the speaker. However, there are times when paraphrasing and feedback are used to create a sense of agreement and approval which comes from Personality's attempt to control and create safety.

Centered Listening is multidimensional. The listener's personal space is expanded to include the speaker which in and of

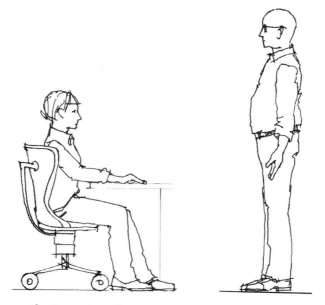

**4b-** Examples of Listening in Center posture

itself creates a good connection. When a listener is Centered, whatever unfolds in the conversation can be appreciated and examined without the agenda of having to establish a good connection. Centered Listening naturally invites the whole of what is being said (verbal and non-verbal) with the inclusiveness of expanded personal space. The need to "get it right" is suspended and there is openness and curiosity regarding the situation. Centered Listening is not invested in getting a particular result, like making the speaker feel accepted or the listener feel they are gathering the right in formation. Centered Listening can tolerate not-knowing and not-understanding. Centered listening includes an exchange of information without the need to get something else from the interaction.

What we hear is only one part of a story. There may be cultural biases against saying what you think because that is considered rude. In such cultures, a person would never be so blunt as to say what they wanted directly. Some people have been conditioned by experiences in which it was dangerous to be direct and outspoken. There are times when the message from the body is different from the verbal content. The words might say, "I am looking forward to the next meeting" while the body, through a tight, constricted posture, communicates the opposite message, "I am not looking forward to the next meeting."

In Centered Listening, we listen for what is *not* being said–by attending to what is underneath the words, what is omitted, and body language so that we can participate in the whole of the communication and fully participate in the exchange. In all communications, it is really important to listen and be open to what is inferred, not just the words.

## Difficult Conversations

When you have a preconceived idea about how a conversation should go or when you become anxious, irritated, or zoned out, or when you are impatient with what someone is saying, you can bet you are in Personality. You may feel stressed because the information is not what you want to hear. Sometimes, the details of what you are hearing may seem wrong or simply inane which stimulates a reaction to stop listening or cut the speaker off. If you sense that the speaker is criticizing you, your defense mechanisms may kick in or you may even begin to criticize yourself. These Personality reactions diminish your ability to receive, assess, and process information.

In Personality's reactive state, our muscles contract. This type of constriction creates separation between listener and

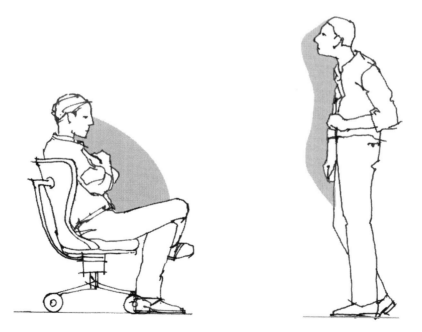

**4c-** Examples of Postural and Personal Space constriction

speaker. This loss of connection and activation of reactivity amplifies the desire for security in both speaker and listener. Remember that Personality's desire to manage the situation can be seen in one's posture.

When we consider the listener's Personality posture, we see these management attempts that can be related to the position the Head, Heart, and Core:

- Control, or trying to make sure that the conversation does not get out of control, is seen in the orientation of the head.

- Approval, or making sure that the speaker thinks he or she is understood, is corroborated by the subservient attitude displayed by chest and arms.

- Safety—by creating the notion that the listener agrees with the speaker which is displayed in compliant the stance of the pelvis and legs.

During difficult conversations, you may find yourself crossing your arms or legs and your breath may become short and tight. When the body contracts, so does the mind. As the mind contracts, the part of the brain that governs big picture thinking, creativity, and innovation begins to shut down and more primitive survival behaviors—variants of fight, flight, and freeze—kick in.

In spite of your survival reactions, you probably will not leap across the table and grab the speaker by the throat or run out of the room. Usually, we have enough cognitive control to recognize the career limitations and social unacceptability of these moves! Nevertheless, stress hormones have prepared your body for fight, flight, or freeze, thus limiting the flexibility of your potential responses. Sitting or standing with constricted muscles, even for just a few minutes, can alter your brain functioning, which in turn alters how you think and speak.

The subtle and not-so-subtle ways that fight, flight, and freeze show up in corporate settings is endless: you freeze up in the middle of a critical business presentation; extricate yourself from an unsafe interaction by agreeing to do something you do not intend to do; say something sarcastic or mean; devise a legitimate reason to leave the meeting early; and on and on.

Once your sensibilities have been hijacked by full-on stress, trying to talk yourself down is a highly inefficient coping mechanism. Internally, you are likely to hear yourself saying, "Don't do it," while you observe yourself continuing to be reactive, despite your better judgment. In stressful situations, employing Centered Listening techniques is a more direct and effective approach to changing your state-of-being. While stress activates the reactive sympathetic nervous system, Centering and adjusting one's posture activates the calming, parasympathetic nervous system.

## Information Lands in the Space

Speakers are often trying to convince the listener about something—they are building a case and want the listener to agree with them. When you listen from Personality, you may be connecting with the speaker's desire to convince. You may be relating unconsciously to times when you were speaking and wanted agreement. Instead of really being interested in the information, you become affected by the need of the speaker to have you agree with them. The speaker may sense the increased desire for agreement, fueling his or her need to have you support them. This Personality type of listening is based on the belief that forming a connection and getting agreement is the most important part of the interaction. When listening from

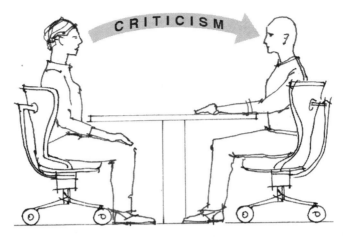

**4d-** Listening from Personality

Personality, you may internalize the content or have the sensation of the words hitting you.

Listening from Personality distracts us from skillfully examining and processing information. With Centered Listening, you see or sense that the words are landing in the space in front of you and you can be more interested and curious about the what is being said, rather than distracted by either the speaker's or your need to reach approval and agreement. With the content and data sitting in front of you, Centered Listening also gives you distance from your own history regarding the material. When a speaker is criticizing you, Centered Listening gives you a way to become interested rather than defensive.

When using Centered Listening, attention is focused on inviting the words and content to land on the table or in the space in front of you, between the speaker and listener. Rather than taking what is being said personally and having the words land on you or internalizing them, you can use Centered Listening

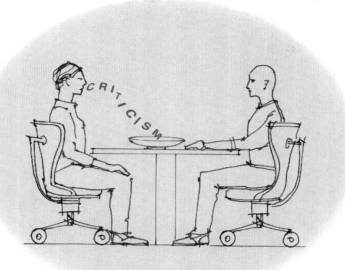

**4e-** Listening from Center

to have the content of what the speaker is saying to actually land outside of you.

In the next exercise, you will experience Centered Listening as both speaker and listener. You will gain a felt-sense of how Centered Listening allows you to receive and process difficult or large amounts of information.

During this exercise, both listener and speaker are to pay attention to how Centered Listening influences their experience of the conversation. You will gain experience in how Centered Listening creates a supportive atmosphere for the exchange of information for both the listener and the speaker. As you continue to practice Centered Listening, you can start using it in your daily conversations and notice what happens.

EXERCISE 7

# Listening from Personality and Center

To begin, choose any topic that is meaningful for you to explore. In the following example, we will use the topic, "Working with Criticism."

## Listening from Personality:

- Sit across from your practice partner so you are facing each other. Your partner will be your stress simulator.

- Give your partner a topic and an example of the content. Choose something that is somewhat difficult but not extremely upsetting. For example, I might ask my partner to say, "This process is not well thought out, I wish you had given us more background information. This feels like a waste of time."

- Now, sit in a closed, stiff, or slightly slumped posture that is indicative of your Personality pattern of constriction in the face of criticism.

- Invite your partner to say the criticism using the content you have suggested.

- Notice how your body responded and ask:

    Did the tightness in my body increase?

    Was there a sense of separation?

    Did I have an impulse to defend and/or attack?

    What other things did I experience in my body?

In my own case, I usually criticize myself first, "Oh, I failed again." And then, I criticize the other person, "She isn't willing to participate, she hasn't even given it a chance." These are typical thoughts I have during my Personality's reaction to being criticized. Can you recognize your Personality's typical reaction?

## Listening from Center:

Now repeat the sequence but, this time, take a moment to Center first.

- Inhale and lengthen your spine, exhale and relax your jaw, shoulders and chest.

- Extend your personal space to the far corners of the room, including your partner.

- Put your attention on the space in front of you and between you and your partner. This is where you will see or sense your partner's words landing outside of you. If you are sitting at a table, you can imagine that the words are landing on the table.

- When you are ready, use a nod or word to signal your partner to begin. Your partner's task is to say the same criticism again, in the same tone and manner and as close to the original statement as possible.

- This time, instead of the words landing on you, see the words landing in space between the two of you so that you can look at then from a distance. This gives you the space to be interested in what is being said. Ask yourself and consider your answers:
  - Is there any value in the criticism?
  - Are any aspects of the criticism helpful to me?
  - Are any elements of the criticism useful as we work together going forward?

Reflect on what happened in your body and ask:
- Was there any lessening of the constriction in my muscles?
- Was I able to breathe more easily?
- What other changes happened in my body?

## Speaker's Centered Listening Experience:

With Centered Listening, you are able to actually listen to the whole of what is being said because you are receptive, yet not taking it personally. You can learn a great deal about Centered Listening when you are the one giving the criticism. So when you are the speaker and the stress simulator, pay attention to what you experience.

- Notice any variations in your state of being as the speaker or stress simulator.

- Consider any differences you experience in yourself as your partner listens from Personality and Center.

- What is it like to say something when the other person is really considering the information rather than reacting to your need to be accepted?

- Does their Centered Listening make you more aware of what you are saying?

The more you practice this listening exercise, the more effective you will be as a communicator and leader. As you speak, when your partner is centered, you feel the stabilizing effect Center. When both speaker and listener are centered, the best possible communication happens. We will more fully explore centered speaking in the next chapter *Speaking Up*.

## *Over Engaging When Listening*

Now, we will look at some of the common non-verbal behaviors that affect the outcome of what is being communicated. When the listener is hooked into the speaker, there is a tendency to create safety by placing more value on making the speaker comfortable than on being open and interested in what is being said. In LE, we call this "over engaging when listening."

The postures and gestures of over engaging include nodding, leaning forward, and unbroken eye contact. You may have noticed these when you or other people were listening intently. They are Personality habits.

Nodding is the most common gesture or pattern in over-engaging. Not the occasional nod, but continuous nodding. Nodding is a non-verbal statement or signal of agreement. Nodding is used to affirm for the speaker that the listener is connected to and supporting them. Some people promote nodding as a way to be a better listener. I am suggesting something altogether different is going on.

When the listener is continuously nodding, he or she is filling the shared space with the non-verbal statement, "Yes, yes, yes...I agree with you." This implied agreement distracts from the communication. Repetitious nodding gives the impression that the listener agrees with the speaker and therefore is not really listening or actually considering what the speaker is saying—as if the listener already knows what the speaker will say before he or she has finished talking. A constantly nodding listener forfeits the sense of wonder and true interest in the communication by already being in agreement with the speaker. What would it be like if you could listen to what is being said as if it were very interesting and worthy of your careful consideration, rather than nodding yes, yes in agreement? In LE trainings, we flush out our reactive Personality listening patterns and practice shifting to Centered Listening.

Two other common patterns of over engaging are a forward leaning posture and unbroken eye contact. Some people think these habits imply that we are intently listening. Again, I suggest that something altogether different is going on.

The habit of leaning forward tends to compress or narrow the shared environment. When we close in the space, we may be attempting to make the speaker feel important, as if the information is a secret—that you do not want others to hear, or that you think that the information is especially noteworthy. With Centered Listening, we make room for information to land in the space between listener and speaker so that it can be more fully heard and explored. LE cultivates the ability to more fully consider what is being communicated by shifting to Center and expanding our personal space, rather than closing in on the speaker.

Some people believe keeping constant eye contact shows that one is paying attention to the speaker. And, many people are comfortable keeping eye contact. While I am sure it is possible to be thoughtful about information and keep eye contact with the speaker, I have found that we can more fully consider information if we break eye contact.

Recall what happens when someone says something that you have not considered before. Do you take a moment to imagine the consequences of applying that information? When you do take that moment, do you continue to look into the eyes of the speaker? Or, do you shift your gaze into the space or make soft eyes, in order to process and explore the implications of the information? Do you take a few moments to embody your considerations? Staring into another person's eyes makes it difficult get a panoramic view of the circumstances. In LE trainings, we practice Centered Listening techniques that allow us to experience more possibilities so that we may choose to be responsive rather than reactive.

## Under Engaging when Listening

Under engaging is a way of attempting to free oneself from the situation. As a form of the primitive flight pattern in current culture, under engaging has evolved to meet cultural requirements of politeness. Instead of running away, the listener's body contracts and attention moves to his or her personal discomfort or concerns, rather than focusing on what the speaker is saying.

In extreme under engaging, a listener's withdrawal can cause the speaker's information to be ignored. A less extreme form of under engaging involves pulling in one's personal space and making it smaller. In some cases, under engaging is an attempt to create a feeling of safety by engaging at an intellectual level while closing down emotionally and nullifying the body's felt-sense. In all forms of under engaging, the listener looses the embodied connection with the speaker and what is being said.

I worked with a scientist who was very smart. When we discussed different ways of listening, he would sit slightly hunched with his arms folded and leaning on the table. I could see that everything I was saying was being processed by his head alone. This scientist would nod at times and I could tell he was thinking about my suggestions, but his body was shut down. My sense was that he was receiving my suggestions as abstract ideas without any embodied experience of them, thus missing both the depth of connection and the usefulness of the content.

Continually striving to acquire more and more information is one way that the Personality's need for safety shows up. Information becomes the currency for safety—the more information that is amassed and processed, the greater the sense of control. Personality defensively flexes muscles that cause a constriction of personal space and excludes others.

## What Shape is Your Body Taking?

As you become more conscious of body language you will

notice that various messages are communicated by body shape and posture. Body patterns that indicate over engaging are leaning forward, continuous nodding, and unbroken eye contact. Body patterns that point to under engaging include crossed arms and/or legs, hunching, shallow breathing, and head bent toward the chest.

Listening from center is based on openness with the exchange of information being only part of the communication. Centered listening is like breathing: we inhale and take in information, process it, and exhale and respond in a way that may involve taking action. Genuine communication makes our world go round—we listen, read, and watch; then we speak, write, and act; then we listen; then we act... Communication is an exchange between people. Sometimes communication is verbal and explicit, and sometimes it is non-verbal and implicit. Most of the time communication is a combination of both.

Body patterns that indicate Centered Listening include: upright and dignified posture, expanded and inclusive personal space, and extended arm positions. When we sit and stand utilizing Centered Listening body postures, our minds become more open and expansive, thereby changing the way we think and speak.

When we are in conversation, in person, on the phone, by text or email, we are both talking and listening—we are sending and receiving information. Centered Listening gives us space to process information and choose how to respond. Centered Listening is a technique to help you be a more skillful and effective listener—how you listen determines how you will speak.

Even though Centered Listening facilitates deeper understanding and connection through being present with the speaker, there are times when the conversation will not yield a positive outcome. You may strongly disagree with the speaker. When a conflict of opinion has strong, deep roots there are no easy fixes. You can hold your position, give in, or adapt. Centered Listening encourages the ability to adapt and move forward—leading to creative outcomes.

# FIVE

# Speaking Up

When we speak our truth, stand behind what we believe, and advance our ideas, we move into the territories of individuation and action. Speaking Up requires a shift from a receptive state of being to an action state. Effective leaders create a felt-sense of belonging, are open to receiving information, and foster collaboration. They then shift to being decisive, saying what needs to happen, and mobilizing their team, family, or group into action that gets the project done.

The shift from collaboration to individuation is not abrupt—it is like breathing, in which we inhale and then exhale, first one then the other, not both at the same time. Likewise, skillful leaders cycle from listening to speaking their truth to inclusive collaboration to decisive action to inclusiveness to individuation to collaboration to receiving feedback to giving directives . . . Embodied leadership is not an either-or. Leadership embodiment is a blend that flows and shifts back and forth between receptivity and advancement.

Speaking Up involves shaping and expanding our personal space into a wedge; aligning and unifying our Head, Heart, and Core; receiving inspiration; and making a declaration. We use LE techniques to prepare for and support us in Speaking Up. We use the shape of our personal space to help us make the shift from receptive to active. In LE trainings, we practice shifting the shape of our personal space back and forth between the circle and the triangle.

## Shaping Personal Space

The shape we give our personal space supports our intentions. Our Personal Space is pliable and changes shape even when we are not aware of it. In LE trainings, we consciously focus our attention on changing the shape of our Personal Space to enhance our leadership presence. Expanding one's personal space into either a sphere or a wedge can be inclusive.

When we expand our personal space into a flexible sphere or circle, it encourages Inclusiveness and Centered Listening and it creates an atmosphere and felt-sense of connection, contribution, and collaboration.

**5a-** Sphere of Expanded Personal Space

When we shape our Personal Space into a dynamic wedge or triangle, we can expand it to be inclusive—even though it is an active shape. The wedge can function as a container for the leader and the team to carry and advance their intentions. The triangle supports our ability to Speaking Up and actively stand behind what we are saying.

The wedge shape provides a vehicle for precise, sharply focused action—moving people and things along, even with resistance, without aggression and without collapse.

**5b-** Wedge of Expanded Personal Space

Moving efficiently through space or matter requires the sharp point and leading edge of a triangle. Think of the way a sharp knife easily cuts through a large carrot or how the shape of the bow of a boat moves through water. We can give our personal space the shape of a triangle to skillfully advance our ideas and actions, even when we encounter resistance.

In LE trainings, we study how the shape of our personal space influences our embodiment of communication. We practice shifting our personal space back and forth between a round, feminine, receptive shape and a sharp, masculine, active shape. Listening and speaking are the feminine and masculine embodiments of communication. Speaking Up is an action that requires a masculine dynamic that can cut through space, matter, and resistance. Speaking Up is an act of personal power, a willingness to take a stand, and stand alone if necessary, in order to manifest what we believe in. When we take a stand and are willing to speak up for truth, even if others do not support our view—we are stepping into our power.

## Implications of Power

The word power has a tendency to trigger negative connotations. For some, power is linked with dominance, aggression, and coldness. For others, power is associated with clarity, focus, and warmth.

All kinds of power activities are at play on the Aikido mat. Here are just a few power examples of the different qualities of power.

| Warm: | Cold: |
|---|---|
| Soft Power | Dominant Power |
| Bright Power | Dark Power |
| Focused Power | Chaotic Power |

An example of soft power can be found in opera where the term "piano" means soft. For a soft sound to carry through a huge opera house, it must be powerful. How is it that an opera singer can softly sing a note that can be heard throughout an expansive space? With LE, we explore ways of speaking that are both soft and powerful at the same time.

The opposite of soft power is dominant power. The quality of soft power invites one to listen while dominant power forces sound onto the listener. Dominant power demands that you listen.

Bright power can be exemplified by gradations of light. At night, stadium lights can be so bright that they light up massive playing fields. Under stadium lights, the flame of a candle does not seem particularly bright. Yet, in a small dark room, the light from a single candle seems bright. LE techniques shift the way we sit and stand which shifts the way we think and speak to brighten up our discussions.

The opposite of bright power is dark power. We have all experienced dark power when we have been around a person who is in a bad mood. The bad mood may be conveyed by an overriding sense of irritation or weariness and a heavy, dreary voice. There can also be a sense of retribution should one not agree with the moody person. A metaphor for dark power is a low ceiling of dark clouds.

Focused power and chaotic power are opposites. Focused power can be seen in the way that a laser organizes light. A laser collects and concentrates light into a single beam. Focused power is clean and clear and conveys the essential quality of its intention. Chaotic power is fractured and scattered. This lack of cohesiveness in chaotic power diffuses the message and frequently creates contradictory information that produces confusion and frustration from the lack of clarity.

## Taking A Stand

When I think about leaders who have spearheaded great change, leaders like Gandhi, Mother Theresa, Martin Luther King, and Nelson Mandela, it is obvious that one of the things they share is a complete commitment to their vision. When we see clips of great leaders, it is clear that every fiber of their being is fully engaged with their words and their actions. They are willing to speak up, take a stand, and give a hundred percent of themselves to support what they believe to be true. They are not self-conscious and they do not hesitate, even in the face of extreme negativity and violent reactions. This level of clarity and commitment springs from a unification and alignment of Head, Heart, and Core that is represented in the synchronization of all aspects of thought and emotion, and a deep desire to act on behalf of others.

Having a willingness to clearly articulate what you stand for is central to embodied leadership. Take a moment now to consider something that is so important and inspiring to you that you would be willing to "take a stand" for it. What is so meaningful to you that you are willing to "stand alone" if necessary? What would you be willing to support even if you were criticized or ridiculed for holding your position?

Now consider some of your experiences with Speaking Up. Think of a time when you spoke up for something and there was a positive response to what you said. What were the circumstances of that situation? Were you attached to the result? Were you self-conscious or afraid of hurting someone's feelings? Or, did you have the sense that no matter what other people said or did, you were still committed to your truth and your actions? If you said yes to this last possibility, you were most likely unified in taking your stand.

Now think of another time when you spoke up and something about it was not right. Maybe you just did not feel good about it. Perhaps you even experienced a negative result. Were you less than one hundred percent on board with yourself or your belief? Where you concerned with how the other person would take it? If so, you were probably split and not unified.

In order to take a stand and speak up for what you believe in, you need to be committed to your intention--not only in your head, but also in your heart and your core—in other words, you need to be unified. Great leaders fully embody their truth.

**5c-** Example of Split posture    **5d-** Example of Unified posture

## *Splits versus Unity*

Rather than teaching us to be unified in the way we interact with others and the world around us, Western culture tends to cultivate divisions in how we relate to the complexity of our lives. At school, we are taught to use our head to be rational, intellectual, and data-driven. With our friends and family, we are expected to be heartfelt and driven by our feelings and emotions. In sports, we are trained to be tenacious and persistent, and "power through it." When there is violence or aggression in the home, we develop an observer, a part of ourselves that is on high alert, so that we can flee from the situation or defend ourselves as needed. These experiences cultivate reactive patterns and create divisions within us. We develop habits of relating to specific situations with different parts of ourselves. In LE, we call this the habit of being split.

Unification brings every part of ourselves to the table. When we are unified our thoughts, feelings, gestures, and breath are coordinated and all parts of ourselves work together. We are congruent, clear, and unified. A unified, embodied leader is a skillful, powerful, and compassionate leader.

## *Creating A Declaration*

When we speak, our state of being organizes around what is most articulate. In LE trainings, we develop clear and concise verbal declarations of what we want to bring into the world. These declarations are spoken out loud to build energy, unification, and momentum for what is to be accomplished. When you say your declaration out loud you send it outside of yourself and into the environment.

People often express what they do not like in a full, emphatic voice, but when it comes time to say what they want to accomplish, their voice lacks energy and their tone is tentative. If given an assignment to have lunch with a friend or colleague and only speak about what is irritating or annoying for a half hour without repeating one's self, most people would pass with flying colors. If, on the other hand, given an assignment to have lunch and only speak about what is exciting and inspiring for a half hour without repeating one's self, most people would have trouble successfully completing the assignment.

Generally, people have more words to describe situations that irritate or disturb them than words to describe what inspires and uplifts them. Our news is dominated by stories and images of crime, devastation, and catastrophe at home and all over the world. Every now and then there is a story about something positive and inspiring, but the negative stories far outnumber the positive. This tendency to focus on problems has resulted in our having a larger vocabulary for describing problems and negativity than for solutions and inspiration.

LE declarations encourage a wide range of inspiring, positive, and powerful expression from specific, discrete goals to proclamations of values to sweeping statements of loving kindness . . . LE declarations are forbearers of what the leader wants to bring into the world. A LE declaration is a sentence or phrase that is concise and easy to say. To utilize your declaration in developing leadership skills, it must sound and feel right when you say it out loud. When you articulate your declaration with a powerful, clear voice, you unify yourself and send your intention out into the world.

Here are some examples of declarations that can be edited or modified to fit your situation.

- I am committed to bringing LE techniques into the world so that everybody has access to them.

- I am committed to having a positive attitude and completing this project on time.

- I am willing to invite support and collaboration from my colleagues to complete this project.

If you are not sure exactly what it is or how you want to say it, then you can use a more generic statement like:

- I am committed to making a contribution.

Creating a declaration is the first step in developing your capacity to speak up and take a stand. You must be willing to change and adjust your declarations as your circumstances change so they are current and applicable for your life right now. Keep your declarations fresh and alive. Update your declarations to keep them current. LE declarations are always works in progress.

The second step in Speaking Up is to identify your sources of inspiration. Who are the leaders that you admire and respect? What is so inspiring that you feel energized to do what it takes to bring it into the world? Organizations have mission statements that function as declarations of what they want to achieve. These declarations are intended to energize and inspire the people who are part of that group. When people in a group are unified with a declaration, they develop a collaborative spirit to work together as a team.

Usually organizations have a mission statement that states the usefulness and value of a service or product. In other words, the people who work in that organization, not only work to produce a service or product, they also work on behalf of those who use the service or product. Think of all the people who will benefit from the service or product that your organization offers. The benefit that those people receive from what your organization produces can be part of your inspiration.

You can also draw inspiration from teachers, mentors, archetypes, and nature. I draw my inspiration from many sources, but I use three primary archetypes. I call them my "posse" which is defined by Webster's dictionary as: "A large group often with a common interest." I use a different archetype for each of my three centers as I invite: the strength and confidence of the founder of Aikido, Morihei Ueshiba, to come through my Core; the compassion of Mother Teresa to come through my Heart; and the wisdom of the Dalai Lama to come through my Head. To be clear, I am not inviting them as actual people. I am relating to the felt-sense of confidence, compassion and wisdom that each of these people inspires in me. People engaged in the LE process have used family members, friends, ancestors, historical figures, and great leaders, for inspiration. The key is to use exemplars of the values and qualities that you want to embody, those with whom you personally resonate.

I also invite elements from nature to be in my inspirational posse. I invite: the strength and uplifting heights of my favorite mountain to come through my Core; the fluid expansiveness of the ocean to come through my Heart; and the clarity and openness of the sky to come through my Head. Additionally, people engaged in the LE process have used flora and fauna for inspiration. Some examples are the majesty of the redwood tree, the courage of the tiger, and the vision of the eagle.

There are many possibilities for inspiration. You can be inspired by people, things and places. Thinking about ancestors, mentors, and the people who will benefit from your company's service or product, can encourage you. The most powerful sources of inspiration come from whatever moves you from "me" to "we." When you do this, you can shift your inner voice from, "I have to do this" to "I am part of a team that has the potential to produce a product or strengthen a community that will be of benefit others."

The point is that your inspiration and posse are available to you any time and any place. Our inspiration and posses serve us in stressful and difficult situations and they can also help to enrich our creative activities and the enjoyment of life.

The next exercise will cultivate a felt-sense of support for Speaking Up, taking a stand, and advancing your intentions.

EXERCISE 8

# Developing a Felt-Sense of Support

- Center:

    1. Inhale up and lengthen your spine.

    2. Exhale and relax your shoulders and soften your chest.

    3. Settle with gravity.

    4. Evoke a quality.

- Extend your arms with elbows straight, not bent.

- Give your personal space a wedge shape.

- Extend the point of the wedge way out in front of you.

- Imagine that the sides of the wedge are sleek and smooth.

- Extend the back of the wedge far out behind you so that you are in the center of the wedge.

- Think of the back part of the wedge as porous, like a colander.

- SAY YOUR DECLARATION OUT LOUD.

- Invite your posse and inspiration to energize you.

- Think of the sensations that come from wind, waves, or hands on your back.

- Imagine that you are receiving a gentle push forward.

- When you can imagine or sense a flow of energy coming through you, look forward—way beyond the tip of the wedge.

- Center: Inhale up, Exhale down, Settle, Evoke a Quality.

- REAFFIRM YOUR DECLARATION OUT LOUD.

- Experience strength and power of advancing your intention with a sense of support and ease, but without aggression or collapse.

**5e-** Receiving Inspiration and Support

## *Learning to Speak Up Without Aggression*

Once you have established your declaration and identified your posse, you can begin the LE exercise of proclaiming your declaration in a simulator that provides the experience of resistance and conflict. Speaking one's truth in a supportive environment is a good practice, but not all that challenging. When people are smiling and applauding, it is easy to feel confident. But what about the times when we experience push back and resistance?

In the next exercise you will use a partner to simulate resistance using mild physical pressure. The purpose of this exercise is to identify and examine your personality's reaction in the face of resistance and conflict while you are trying to move forward with your declaration.

EXERCISE 9

# Partner Resistance to Identify Personality Pattern

*1. Make sure that your partner holds your forearms slightly above your wrist joints so that the resistive pressure and impact goes into the forearms and not into the wrist joints.

2. The pressure should be mild to medium and gently sustained, NOT hard or rough.

**5f-** Form a Triangle with body, top view

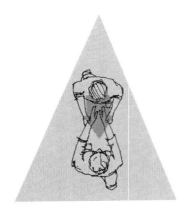

**5g-** Expand PS into wedge while partner sustains pressure, top view

- Stand so you and your partner are facing each other.

- Put one foot forward, raise your arms in front of you and put your palms together so your arms and the back of your body form the shape of a triangle.

- Focus you attention on your Personal Space and shape it into a triangle using the back of your body and your arms to mark the constricted boundaries of your personal space.

- Ask your partner to take hold of your forearms* and apply mild to medium resistive pressure.

- Say your declaration out loud to you partner, then attempt to step forward. Your partner will continue to keep applying the resistive pressure.

- Notice what you do with your arms and torso and ask: What are the shape of my arms and the bend in my elbows? Is there any constriction or collapsing in my torso? Am I pushing back? Am I pulling away?

Generally, we have three possible responses to dealing with resistance – we can steamroll, get stuck or give up. Often the Personality pattern here is the same or similar to what showed up in the earlier partner exercises. In my case, my head and shoulders go forward and my hips go back in quick succession. I steamroll and then give up.

The more quickly and clearly you can recognize your pattern arising, the easier it will be to shift to a centered way of being when meeting challenge. Ignoring or covering up a pattern takes a lot of energy which reduces the vitality that you have to give to your project. For example, the General Council of an organization that I worked with had a pattern of sitting slightly slouched with both her arms and her legs crossed. This posture requires a great deal of muscle constriction. During her attempts to get her point across, she would talk in a loud and aggressive voice. The combination of a constricted body and an aggressive voice stimulated negative reactions in the other people in the meeting—her posture and voice triggered resistance in them. They became less receptive and more resistive to what she was saying, which resulted in longer arguments that significantly extended the time it took to resolve issues.

When we study our Personality reactions to intensity, impact, and resistance, what shows up over and over again is the constriction of muscles, shallow breathing, and the narrowing of perception. In other words, we lose access to information, creative potential, and the big picture.

In his article, *The Basics of Quantum Healing*, (http://ascension-research.org/reality.html), Dr. Deepak Chopra, says it this way:

> "We link stimuli to certain memories and every time we're exposed to those stimuli we reinterpret the universe and ourselves according to the memories. We become the victim of the stale repetition of outworn memories. So through the same mechanics we keep creating and become bundles of conditioned reflexes and responses constantly being triggered by people and circumstance into the same predictable biochemical responses and ultimately into the same behavioral responses."

Practicing a more expansive response while using a resistance simulator gives your nervous system and your muscles the embodied experience of shifting from reactive to responsive. Rather than being stuck in your reactions, you develop responsive choices. When you Speak Up from a centered way of being, you train your body to be responsive, which shifts your biochemistry thereby allowing your brain to access a more expansive perception that gives you a choice of responses.

The next exercise lets you experience the difference between Speaking Up from Personality and Speaking Up from Center. You will continue to use the shape of the triangle. This time you will expand your triangular Personal Space so it is large enough to include both you and your partner.

EXERCISE 10

# Shifting from Personality to Center
# with Resistance

- Repeat the previous exercise, "Partner Resistance to Identify Personality Pattern."

- Experience and acknowledge your Personality Pattern.

- Ask your partner to provide and sustain steady resistance throughout the exercise.

- Center:

    1. Inhale and lengthen your spine.

    2. Exhale and relax your shoulders and soften your chest.

    3. Settle with gravity.

    4. Evoke a quality.

- Your partner continues to sustain steady pressure.

- Extend your arms so that your elbows are straight and not bent.

- Bend your front knee a little and settle onto your front leg.

- Use your imagination to shape your Personal Space into a wedge.

- Extend the point or leading edge of the wedge out, way beyond your partner.

- Extend the flat part of the wedge equally far behind you.

- Think of the back part of the wedge as porous like a colander.

(continued)

EXERCISE 10 (continued)

• SAY YOUR DECLARATION OUT LOUD.

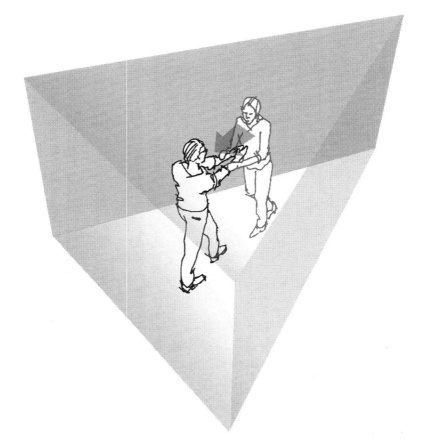

**5h-** PS Wedge and Sustained Pressure

• Invite your posse and inspiration to energize and support you.

• Think of a sensation like a wind, a wave, or hands on your back giving you a gentle push forward.

**5i-** Posse supports you moving forward

- When you can imagine or sense a burst of energy flowing through you, look forward beyond your partner and his or her steady resistance.

- Stand upright, and without leaning into the resistance take three steps forward keeping you attention on the sense of inspiration that is coming through you and beyond you.

- Experience the strength and power of advancing with ease, and without aggression, when there is resistance.

This exercise is designed to mimic the experience of being in the "zone" or "flow state." You are re-enacting those moments when suddenly an activity became easier, when the way seemed clear and you experienced a sense of flow rather than effort. It is essential that your body gets a clear imprint of the difference between Speaking Up from Personality, with the sense of being a separate individual attempting to push through resistance on your own, and Speaking Up from Center, with the sense of being part of a collective that is working together and having the ability to call up resources and support from the environment in the moment.

Your mental habits and belief system, can make it more or less difficult to experience yourself as supported and energized by archetypes or a collective. Our family of origin, our education, the community we grew up in, and our life experience together form our beliefs about how much things are connected or separated. Generally in Western culture we are taught that we are separate individuals capable of connecting with others by virtue of conscious recognition and attention to another person. There is an implication that to maintain a connection, we must continuously acknowledge and verify each other.

Another way to look at relationship is to regard each other as part of a whole that is interconnected, intelligent, and self-organizing, rather than thinking that we are separate individuals managing our lives solely through our own volition. That may sound far-fetched but it is a descriptive scientific perspective. We may be in the habit of experiencing ourselves as separate but that does not make it true or helpful.

There is tremendous value in being flexible and adaptive. Having the capacity to experience your interactions as a part of a connected, self-organizing, intelligent whole, while simultaneously experiencing your individual personal journey, is the hallmark of an adaptive, creative, and mature leader. The more this type of leader continues to develop his or her abilities for Inclusiveness, Centered Listening, and Speaking Up the more powerful he or she becomes. The embodied leader develops a magnetic quality that communicates a message of possibility and contribution and inspires teamwork.

No matter how mature and agile we become as leaders, new challenges can still trigger our Personality to arise. Our body will still react with its survival pattern—putting up a boundary and constricting—just like you experienced it in the "Partner Front Push" exercise when pressure is applied quickly to your forearms. You must be vigilant and mindful in order to recognize when the old patterns begin to arise. Instead of ignoring or overriding Personality survival patterns, you must cultivate a deep respect for them and acknowledge the power of your Personality habit of individuating and protecting.

## Technique: Training Pattern Awareness

An effective way to become more aware of your reactive patterns is to develop a ritual of quickly checking your posture and muscle tension at least ten times a day. Each check-in will only take five to ten seconds—you will check the vertical alignment of your posture and notice which muscle groups you are flexing and extending. When your Head, Heart and Core are not in alignment or you are flexing your back and elbows, you are contracted and in Personality.

If you determine that you are in Personality, you can then shift to Center by using either the five- or twenty-second centering practices. This ritual of checking and shifting will enable you to develop a rigorous yet relaxed self-awareness. Such self-awareness will enhance your ability to shift from Personality to Center more quickly and easily in stressful situations. As these abilities grow and the embodied leader experiences more effectiveness and therefore more recognition, the leader's visibility increases. Next we will examine the challenges that arise with increased visibility.

## Visibility

For the sense in which we use the term visibility, the World English Dictionary defines visibility as: "The degree to which somebody or something is easily noticed by and catches the attention of the public or a particular group of people."

At first blush, the idea of being seen and recognized seems very attractive: what you do becomes noticed and appreciated. However, although it is true that people will see you more, it is not likely that everyone will always appreciate your choices or actions. As you grow in your leadership presence, everything else will grow along with it. You will receive more respect and more envy, more appreciation and more resentment, more responsibility and more pressure to get the job done. Inevitably, people will have varying reactions to the choices you make and how you implement those choices. Remember the line in George Leonard's quote about homeostasis – "…the resistance is equal to the speed and scope of the change…"

When Personality is triggered, there is usually some sort of split or conflict within ourselves as our pattern displays at least two parts of ourselves moving in different directions. Part of the Personality pattern is constricting and separating, which allows us continue our sense of smallness while extending out to relate to the other person or situation. If you look closely, you might see a pattern that translates as "See this part of me, but not that part of me. See what I do, but don't look too closely at me." It is as if you want to keep your privacy and be open and available at the same time. Personality wants to cover up the parts that are vulnerable and impatient—it wants to keep them private. Personality has a preferred image that it wants other people to see—an image that is confident and at ease with responsibility and visibility. But is this really that case?

The problem with leading from Personality is that is takes a great deal of contraction and energy to keep some parts of us hidden while attempting to expose only certain other parts to the world. Added to that, it takes a tremendous amount of energy to maintain the self-consciousness required to be constantly checking other people's responses to see if things are going according to plan. Using all this energy to keep things together can be exhausting and deplete the reserves needed for creativity and collaboration. Operating from Personality could leave less than half of your life force available for your projects. Fortunately you do not have to work from a depleted reserve. Instead you can train yourself to recover and shift from Personality to Center.

Remember, your centered self has access to energy reserves and resources unavailable to your Personality. The centered part of you is connected to the whole and its collective intelligence and creativity. When you Center, you invite inspiration from teachers, mentors, and archetypes into the room. Your centered self has natural confidence because it is not afraid of success or failure. Every great leader has failed, learned from their failures and gone on to adapt and implement the next step to manifest their vision. Personality is afraid of failure and constricts in the face of criticism. But failure is not only inevitable, it is how we learn what we can and cannot do.

Tim Harford in his book, *Adapt: Why Success Always Starts with Failure*, has this to say about the importance of failure: "Here's the thing about failure in innovation: it's a price worth paying. We don't expect every lottery ticket to pay a prize, but if we want any chance of winning that prize, then we buy a ticket. In the statistical jargon, the pattern of innovative returns is heavily skewed to the upside; that means a lot of small failures and a few gigantic successes."

Center is willing to take risks and stay interested. Why? Because when you activate a more dignified and uplifted posture along with a more open and expansive personal space, your chemical balance changes. You begin to manufacture more testosterone, the confidence chemical. Your concern about how others see you becomes muted and your sense of visibility is no longer about how you are seen, but instead it is about what you see. If posture goes beyond dignified and uplifted to aggressive and imposing, this freedom from concern about others' opinions becomes dangerous. From Center, however, we are always balancing our power with an inclusive and curious disposition. We are operating from the sense that "We are all in this together." Our power is in service of bold action, fearlessly leading the group and showing the way.

In order to be empowered and effective as a leader with a clear authentic voice that is connected to truth, you need to be unified and energized. If you notice that the critic or the observer is taking over, you can stop and do a five- or twenty-second centering practice. If you have something to say, focus your personal space into a large triangle and invite support and inspiration. It only takes a few seconds to recover Center and it makes a big difference in your leadership presence.

### The Camry Effect

I was co-leading a workshop called Power and Love, with a friend and colleague, Adam Kahane, when he told this story:

In the 90s, Adam was in South Africa working on the Mont Fleur Scenarios that were supporting Nelson Mandela to become the next leader of South Africa. He needed to buy a car. His father had always owned a Toyota Tercel. Adam was going to stick with the family brand, only he wanted the next step up from the Tercel. The Toyota dealer suggested a Camry, so he purchased one and drove it home. He told us that before he went to the dealer, he had never seen a Camry. Yet, on the way back to his house, he said he saw 20 Camries.

I love this story because it points out that until something is brought to our attention, we often miss the fact that it exists at all. Once something is pointed out, we not only see it, but can include the phenomena in our views of the world and our behavior. And so it is with recognizing how we constrict, disconnect, and individuate when we are stressed and tired. In LE speak, we often refer to waking up to new information that has been there all along, but not seen until pointed out to us, as in the Camry Effect.

The questions below could assist you to see how you may be limiting yourself in regards to visibility. They are designed to promote more awareness of how you experience your visibility profile—what it means "to be seen." Take a few minutes now to consider each of these questions and make written notes of your answers.

What do I want people to see about me?
(List three. Examples: intelligent, confident, considerate)

What do I not want people to see about me?
(List three. Examples: unsure, worried, overwhelmed)

What do I imagine people see about me?
(List three. Examples: dependable, sensitive, hardworking)

How do I keep people from seeing parts of myself that I don't want exposed? (List three. Examples: make jokes, change the subject, talk about what I know)

What are the energetic patterns that I use to keep myself from being visible? (List three. Examples: tight muscles, shallow breathing, slumped posture)

Now that you have written down these things related to your visibility issues, take a moment to reflect and appreciate how your visibility habits have functioned to give you a sense of safety. They are linked to your Personality's survival mechanism. Remember the three centers and their Personality priorities: Head (control), Heart (approval), and Core (safety). Your Personality is attempting to help you avoid the unpleasant and threatening consequences that being more visible could bring, things like overwork, being disliked or envied, having to develop new skills, altering well-established relationships, becoming open to attack, being a target for blame, having your mistakes aired publicly…It is challenging to behave differently while the survival urge works to keep you doing the same old behavior.

There is an exercise for examining your pattern when you greet someone with a handshake. The way we shake hands is a personal pattern like a signature. For instance, when I shake hands, I put my right foot forward with about 60% of my weight on it. I lean forward with my upper body and turn my belly button slightly to the left. My arm has a slight bend at the elbow. In northern European countries, people tend to grip strongly and pump, usually three or four pumps. They may also do a series of small rapid pumps, like a jiggle of the hand.

Once you are aware of your pattern, I suggest you practice centering before a handshake. When standing in front of your partner, do a five- or twenty-second centering, then extend your arm out so that it is mostly straight and take the other person's hand. If you over-squeeze you will cause contraction and both of you will shut down. You will only feel the squeeze, rather than experiencing the sense of connection flowing from your Core. If your grip offers connection, your energy will flow from your core through your arm and hand into the other person and genuine contact is made. There was a woman in one of the LE trainings, who wanted to step to the up next level of leadership at her workplace. During the handshake exercise, her pattern was obvious. She had a very light touch with just her fingers, her weight was on her back foot, and she had a lot of bend in her elbow. She was not engaging much of herself in the handshake, indicating that her Personality was not comfortable with being seen as strong and available. When she practiced shaking hands from Center, she let out a big breath and said, "Oh, this is so intense." My response to her was, "Now is the time for you to be intense and more visible as a leader."

The urge for security is natural and deeply rooted in everyone's psyche. The desire for security is part of what makes us human. Of course, we all want things to be under control, we want people to like us, and we want to be safe. The problem occurs when these desires dominate our behavior. Then, they become more of a liability than an asset. You do not need to transform or repress your survival patterns. Rather, the essential thing is to manage how much time you spend in survival state. The founder of aikido said, "I do get off center, and I correct so fast that no one can see it." Leadership power is in your ability to quickly recover Center, not in your ability to stay there indefinitely. You can develop a habit of quickly shifting to Center by repeatedly using either the five- or twenty-second centering practice throughout each day—especially when you are stressed.

There are many ways that you can learn about yourself. Some organizations conduct 360-degree feedback assessments of their employees, which include of a survey of the employee's boss, peers, direct reports, and customer comments. Although this kind of process can be valuable, it is also possible to see ourselves without that aid, if we examine our posture. The same personality patterns that appear in a 360-degree assessment are also evident in how we hold our bodies. If a person gets the feedback that they need to speak up more, their body posture will often be sitting back with their arms crossed and their head slightly lowered. If the feedback is that a person is too aggressive and does not listen enough, their body posture may exhibit a forward lean and, if sitting at a desk or table, he or she will usually lean on it with their arms.

Another pattern to be aware of is the tendency to become overly engaged with your internal observer. Noticing can be helpful, but when too much attention is diverted to watching yourself, you become self-conscious. In this self-conscious state, part of your presence withdraws and you no longer welcome input nor are you open for expansive inclusiveness. As your observer draws the focus of your attention to how others perceive you—your Head is busy gathering, sorting, assessing, and interpreting those perceptions—you appear to be remote and unavailable, your leadership presence diminishes and you are then perceived as being separate and aloof.

## The Challenge of Success

Years ago, I was leading a course and we were discussing the challenges of success. One of the participants said, "I have no problem with success, I just never get it." So I made up an exercise to study what goes on with success from the point of view of the energetic patterns in our body. What we discovered was that the body cannot always tolerate the amount of energy or intensity that is triggered by the change that success brings to our lives. Material success brings greater visibility and responsibility. Success requires a shift to manage the increased demands on our time and decisions regarding the additional material acquisitions associated with it. We may want to be more successful, but when that success materializes, it is rarely is what we thought it would be.

Wanting success is different than having it. When we think about success, we see the upsides: accolades, status, wealth, power...What we do not necessarily anticipate is the psychological and relational impact success will have. Old friends may feel left behind and drift away, the power in our intimate relationships may shift, people we once reported to may become our employees, the impact of our decisions may have far reaching consequences for an ever-widening circle of people, demands to keep up with our peers intensify, we are expected to maintain an image in keeping with our position...Success alters every part of our existence. Remember the quote about homeostasis? "...the resistance is equal to the speed and scope of the change, not necessarily to whether it is adaptive or maladaptive."

So, how do you work with the phenomenon of success without sabotaging yourself or over working so you do not have to feel the effect of the change? You can prepare for change by practicing the next exercise. Use it when you are thinking of making a change in your habits or life—from little things like always putting your keys where you can find them to big things like accepting a promotion or changing jobs.

EXERCISE 11

# Receiving Success

- Start by imagining yourself being successful in a way that you desire.

- You can start low or high—a little more successful than you are currently or a huge amount success.

- Spend a few moments thinking about the changes that this level of success would bring to your life.

- Notice what you experience in your body when you contemplate this success and ask:

  How is this level of intensity being managed by my nervous system?
  What is happening with my heart rate? How is my breathing?
  What is my capacity for relaxation? What other sensations am I experiencing?

- Now choose a different level of success, up or down from where you started.

- Spend a few moments thinking about the changes that this new level of success would bring to your life.

- Again, notice what you experience in your body when you contemplate the success and ask the same questions as above.

- Continue changing the levels of success and repeat the sequence of imaginative thinking, contemplation, noticing, and inquiry until you find a level of success that your body can tolerate.

- When you have conjured up a tolerable level of success, take a few minutes to fantasize about or imagine the details of what that success would include.

When I do this exercise, I usually start high and move down in successive percentages to discover what intensity of change my body, not my mind, can accept. Some examples of a "high" level of success could be: having a best seller or receiving millions of dollars in funding or speaking to 25,000 people. As ideas, these all sound wonderful. My mind says, "What could be the problem?" But what happens when my body has to manage the energy of such a huge change? The short answer is, it gets overwhelmed.

As a result of being overwhelmed, my unconscious Personality habits will try to find ways to return to what is familiar. In other words, Personality will sabotage me and try to get back to the status quo. So, I take it down a notch and consider success as receiving one-half or two-thirds of the original vision. I check in with my body. How is my nervous system managing this percentage of added intensity? How are my heart rate, my breathing and my capacity for relaxation?

The point is to find the level of change that your body can tolerate, then fantasize or imagine that. You will be much more likely to get what you desire if your body can accept the amount of energy and intensity implied in the change. Once you can live with the intensity of that success without sabotaging it, you can go to the next step. Imagine a little more success, and when you can handle that, imagine little more. . .Before you know it, you will be able to hold your original vision, armed with confidence and resourcefulness.

Becoming aware of your own tendencies and habits of relating to challenges is key to being able to choose an alternative. The practice and observation that are suggested above are designed to clarify what gets in the way of speaking your truth and if necessary, standing alone. Once you see the habits that disempower you, you have taken the first step. Next step is to practice, over and over again, activating an alternative. The LE Centering Practice is the doorway to having choice—inhale and uplift your posture, exhale and relax your shoulders and chest, settle with gravity, and evoke a quality—the more you do it, the easier it is to do it.

## *Empowerment – Standing Alone*

There are many processes and techniques for collaboration and learning to work together. There are not as many practices for how to take a stand and be powerful and autonomous. Both collaboration and Speaking Up are needed to be effective as a leader and an agent of change. There may be times when you cannot convince others to see it your way. You now have some techniques to practice that will help you stay the course and if need be, stay it alone. I once was talking to a friend who is a high level executive of a big company. I was telling him about my next book—this book. He said, "I hope you write a chapter entitled, 'It's lonely at the top.'" Yes, it can be very lonely. You will feel alone if you allow your Personality to dominate your experience. Personality by definition is separate and individuated. When I reminded the executive that he could shift to Center, he brightened up immediately. When you Center, you are never alone. In Center, you have: a big picture point of view, access to collective intelligence and interconnection, and your posse is always there—all of this is ready to energize and support you in advancing your intention while reminding you that—we are all in this together.

# SIX

# Bringing It Together

Now that you have read about LE techniques and have tried out some of the LE exercises, you can begin to integrate LE practices into your daily life. In the previous chapters, we have explored the three leadership competencies of Inclusiveness, Centered Listening and Speaking Up. Although they have been presented individually they naturally work together to promote authentic, compassionate, and powerful leadership.

## *Adjusting, Adapting, and Risk Taking*

We are living in a time of instability, possibility, and change in all aspects of our lives. What will happen and what the future holds is anyone's guess. Leaders need to be smart, intuitive, creative, and most importantly, they need to be able adjust to changing situations. How do you develop your ability to adapt and change in accordance with whatever is arising in the present moment? How do you fully see what is happening? How do you respond to input, data, and empirical information regarding the present situation? How do you prepare for unknown potential?

My answer is that you use LE centering techniques to increase your access to the parts of your brain and body that are capable of responding skillfully and accessing a wide range of resources.

Before we review some of the LE theory and techniques, I will compare two types of leaders: The Expert and The Alchemist.

The Expert leader tends to believe that he or she knows the answers. When you think you know the answers, you can feel secure in believing that you are right. This righteousness gives a sense of being in control—you expect that others will respect you and acquiesce to your expertise. You project the illusion that you, with all your expertness, can safely lead the project to the desired outcome. Sound familiar? This is Personality animated by its overriding desire for control, approval, and safety.

To be an effective leader, you must be more than an expert. When you lead from Center, you become an Alchemist. Alchemy is defined as: *a power or process of transforming something common into something special*. While an Expert references themselves—their experiences and their intellectual data bank, the Alchemist accesses all of that plus a much greater pool of resources from the collective input of their team. Centered leaders can explore a variety of possibilities while tolerating not-knowing the outcome. The Alchemist uses the assets of intuition and innovation that Center offers. Alchemists are willing to dance on the edge—taking risks, failing or succeeding, and adapting in order to advance the project, product, or service. Tim Hartford speaks of this in his book *Adapt*, "Whether we like it or not, trial and error is a tremendously powerful process for solving problems in a complex world, while expert leadership is not."

Peter Palchinsky was a Russian engineer in the 1920s who believed most real-world problems are more complex than they appear. He believed problems have a human dimension and, a local dimension, and that they are likely to change as circumstances change. His method for dealing with this fluctuation is summarized as Palchinsky Principles: first, seek out new ideas and try new things; second, when trying something new, do it on a scale where failure is survivable; and third, seek out feedback and learn from your mistakes as you go along.

### Seek out new ideas and try new things.

Seeking and trying require an open mind and willingness to inquire. For the centered leader, the inquiry is not limited to: How do we get our numbers up? Rather, the questions are: What are we not seeing? What might be possible if we were aware of and addressed the fears that close down the pathways to innovation? How can we further support and inspire the hearts and minds of our team members to engender their eagerness to suggest and explore new things?

Inclusiveness is the container that supports inspiration, innovation, and risk-taking. Isolation and separation are inherently divisive and thwart teamwork. Centered Listening creates an atmosphere for hearing and exploring new things and ideas. Personality is usually closed to suggestions that do not seem highly rational. Center is willing to consider any possibility.

New ideas must be expressed in order to be explored. Anyone who suggests something new or unusual is taking a risk. For those who want to advance beyond existing limits and explore new possibilities, the ability to Speaking Up is essential. Center supports your ability to clearly articulate and stand behind the ideas, behaviors, and actions that you want to bring into the world. Changes are easier to implement if you are centered and operating from that place of openness, presence, and creativity.

### Do it on a scale where failure is survivable.

Of course, your failure scale will depend on the size and resources of your organization. Nonetheless, the point here is that failure becomes acceptable. Our Personality's survival habits are not programmed for failure. Our educational system has programmed to believe that failure is bad and, in some cases, unacceptable. In LE, we redefine failure as a stepping-stone to success. Remember the part of Michael Jordon's wonderful quote where he says, "I've failed over and over and over again in my life. And that is why I succeed."

It takes practice, confidence, and a good deal of concentration to move beyond bias against failure and customs of rewarding success and punishing failure. Center is not constrained by such beliefs. Center can access the confidence, compassion and creativity that is beyond praise and blame because Center is not concerned with what other people think. Rather, Center is open to many possibilities for manifesting contributions for the greater good.

### Seek out feedback and learn from your mistakes as you go along.

Centered Listening helps you to receive feedback more skillfully and gracefully. In his classic book on leadership, *Good to Great*, Jim Collins writes about how a leader's ability to receive hard feedback affects his or her ability to move a company toward greatness. Without feedback, you will be unable to know what is going on and most likely will have trouble in adapting to the ever-changing environment of everyday business. When you use Centered Listening to receive and process feedback, you will be able to make a skillful reply. Sometimes while processing feedback, you may slip into Personality, which is an indication of the tendency to react out of the need for control, approval or safety. LE training invites you to recognize the signs of your Personality patterns so that you can then take a few seconds to shift to Center using the five- or twenty-second centering practices.

## Responding to Feedback – speaking up

As you get ready to respond to feedback, use the five- or twenty-second centering practice. Then check in with yourself to see if you are unified by asking, "Is what I am about to say true in my core and my heart as well as my head? Am I speaking on behalf of the greater good?" If you have been practicing the LE Speaking Up techniques, you will have a felt-sense of whether or not you are unified. If your Head, Heart, and Core are aligned you are ready to speak from Center. If not, shift your posture to vertically align your head, heart and core and center again using the five- or twenty-second centering practice. Then, before you reply, shape your personal space into a large wedge that includes the people to whom you are speaking. Remember, Speaking Up is an action. You are intending to make a point, to make something happen. To be an effective leader, you need to engage all of yourself. Along with the unification of your Head, Heart, and Core, your personal space must be as much a part of you as your flesh and bones. Use your concentration to make the shape of your personal space clear and definite. Take the time to extend your personal space into and then beyond the room. Only then say what is true for you.

## It is all in the Recovery

Of course no one is able to continuously be in Center. There are times when the stakes are so high and he pressure so intense that your concentration and practice will be unable to match the situation. During those times, you will probably react with your well-used reactive habit—your Personality's survival behavior. This is not a problem but rather a normal phase in developing your skills as a leader. You can use such times to remind yourself that you are growing in your ability to act from Center in stressful situations by using a phrase like, "I can't manage this situation from Center yet." The "yet" is the key concept that allows you to recognize that you are growing in your ability to respond from Center. Remember that you are on a path of practice that, little by little, will eventually enable you to shift to Center in stressful situations. Your practice is like growing a muscle and it takes time and repetition to build the strength. As the Greek poet, Archilochos wrote, "Under duress, we don't rise to our expectations. We fall to our level of training." In martial arts training, we do not give up or think a technique has no merit when we can not apply it in practice. Rather, we continue to practice knowing that eventually we will be able to be more open relaxed and fluid while being attacked—we will find the opening, have the timing, and execute the move with ease.

I find it helpful to think of numbers, percentages, and watts when I the practice strengthening my ability to Center under stress. I ask myself, "On a scale of one to 100, what level of intensity is this situation?" Let's say that the circumstance is a 75 watt situation and I can only activate 65 watts of Center, then I will lose Center and revert back to Personality reaction and behavior. If on the other hand, the situation has 50 watts of intensity and I can activate 65 watts of Center, I will probably be able to maintain Center as I listen, speak, and act with clarity and presence. The good news is that life gives us plenty of opportunities to practice, and the more we practice the stronger our ability to Center becomes—we can raise our numbers. With practice, 75 watts of intensity becomes manageable—the bar has been raised and we start practicing for 80 watts!

The concepts and exercises in this book are only a part of the Leadership Embodiment process. A larger body of work and knowledge is available through LE coaching and courses.

Working with the body has become part of mainstream conversations regarding leadership and its role in shaping the future. It takes more than an intellectual understanding to manage the dynamics of complex situations. LE theory is informed by thousands of years old wisdom lineages as well as the latest explorations in the field of neuroscience.

Whatever your entry point, there is a deep reservoir of wisdom, compassion, and power waiting to be tapped by those who are willing to go beyond the data. We now know that we have access to more levels of intelligence if we open and respond to our body's wisdom and intuition, and to collective knowledge.

If we do not examine and own our stress reactions, they will sabotage us. Under duress the body always wins. Recognizing our reactive patterns early gives us the choice to respond. We can choose to uplift, open, and settle in order to get a panoramic view of any situation which enables us to see more options and to find higher quality solutions.

Attaining Center is not a one-time thing—it is something we must practice as much as possible to counter the deep-seated power of our stress reaction. If we practice shifting to Center enough, it will become a habit that gives us more options under stress.

Taking five seconds to Center, ten or twenty times a day, is a quick and easy way for you to cultivate a calm and balanced focus. It may seem like a lot but there are places where that kind of discipline would be just scratching the surface.

When I was in Bhutan I met teachers and practitioners of Vajrayana Bhuddism. To progress along that path of study a student must do 100,000 repetitions of prayer and 100,000 repetitions of prostrations or bowing—this is just to move past the first level! Once 1,000,000 repetitions of both have been reached, around 30 years of 100 repetitions of each per day, it is recommended that a practitioner continue doing at least 100 repetitions daily forever after. Many of the lamas have performed 1,000,000 or more. They believe that the prayers and prostrations are a way of keeping a clear connection to the wisdom, compassion, and power that they aspire to embody. It was a joy to be in their presence. The feeling of openness, kindness, and inclusiveness was palpable.

The ongoing practice of shifting to Center for five seconds, ten or twenty times a day, quickly and easily cultivates your capacity for calm and balanced focus. Five seconds of shifting to Center, twenty times a day takes 100 seconds—just a little more than a minute and a half a day. But remember, it is not just a minute and a half, one time a day—rather, it is five seconds at a time, used twenty times throughout the day. Progress is made, maintained, and gained by continuing to integrate Center, Inclusiveness, Centered Listening, and Speaking Up into our daily lives with short spurts of practice. It is the habit of repetitious practice that advances our skill as embodied leaders.

All this practice may seem like a lot of work, but why not give it a try? Dealing with stress is a lot of work as well, although it may seem easier because we are more accustomed to that kind of work. Perhaps the wisdom traditions are on to something. Perhaps committed ongoing practice can change the neural pathways in our brains. Anyway, it is worth a shot. The amount of time and energy we put into trying to control our lives is huge—clearly it is more efficient to practice shifting to Center and strengthening our ability to respond.

As in all areas of learning and development, there are important elements that are essential to advancement: the material, a coach or knowledgeable person to impart the material, and a learning community, team, or organization to provide ongoing support.

This book offers some of the fundamentals of LE practice and theory. In order to go forward and progress in working with LE techniques, I recommend that you work with a LE coach or teacher. The understanding and experience you gain from a learning community through courses, retreats and practice groups will give you the depth and skill to employ the techniques and theory in an authentic way.

Effective leadership requires engagement of all the pieces that comprise ourselves. The challenges we face as individuals, as communities, and as a global family are awesome. By tapping our true potential, we too can be awesome. We need to engage every fiber of our being if we are going to meet life's challenges. In my windsurfing days, we had a saying: "Satisfaction is being well used." I encourage you to use every bit of yourself to bring about a better world for everyone including the generations that will come after us.

With access to global communication and information just a fingertip away you do not have to go it alone. There are people throughout the world engaged in this work. Many of these people have told me that working with the body has for them been the "missing piece."

Be compassionate with yourself—the habits ingrained over many years will not surrender easily. It takes perseverance, awareness and lots of practice to activate a different way of engaging—yet it can be done. I have witnessed marvelous shifts in the way people sit and stand that have resulted in very different ways of thinking and speaking. This cannot be achieved without practice and repetition. The neural pathways that transmit the impulses triggered by our Personality reactions have deep grooves—established by thousands of repetitions. Yet our bodies have the ability to repair, restore, and regenerate—we can learn to do things differently. The act of shifting to Center is the trigger that can alter the way you respond—change the way you sit and stand and you will change the way you think and speak.

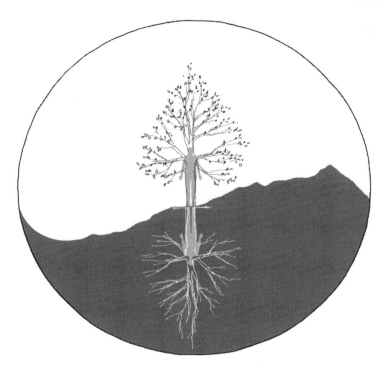

**6a-** Natural Embodiment

Our bodies are deeply affected by natural forces that we often ignore. Nature provides resources that support us in our quest for confidence, stability, compassion, health, and wisdom—enabling us to be of service. Gravity allows us to feel rooted in our sense of belonging. Just as a tree's roots go deep into the earth to nourish and stabilize the trunk and branches—our sense of belonging to the earth encourages our sense of confidence, stability, and health. The centrifugal force that extends outward from a rotating mass, such as the earth, stimulates an upward sensation. Our embodiment of compassion, wisdom, and service can flourish when we cultivate an uplifted and expansive posture—just as the trunk of a tree naturally extends upward, towards the sun.

PART TWO

# The Biology Behind It All

## Janet Crawford

# SEVEN

# Science & Embodiment

My name is Janet Crawford, and my company, Cascadance, specializes in the application of neuroscience and other behavioral disciplines to leadership development and culture design. Our mission is to help organizations achieve excellence through leveraging the best in human biology.

When I was first introduced to somatic practices like the ones contained in this book, I was fascinated. The changes I saw in my own life were exhilarating. Secretly, though, I wondered how I could introduce the practices to my corporate clients. I feared that they might reject them as too ungrounded, "new age," or "touchy-feely."

Admittedly, this was many years ago. Somatic practices have now gained some degree of mainstream resonance. To this day, however, I still occasionally encounter puzzled looks and what I call the "huh?!" reaction. More often, leaders have an intuition that Leadership Embodiment practices have merit, but struggle to justify investing the time and energy to learn and practice them. In Western business culture, after all, we conflate understanding with the ability to act and believe that logic and words should be enough to influence.

Over the past decade and a half of delving deep into the science of human behavior, I have realized that neuroscience provides a perfect bridge between the hyper-rationality of the typical Western workplace and these much needed tools for expanding leadership effectiveness and presence.

A disclaimer: I am trained as a scientist, but I am not, as many people assume, a neuroscientist. I grew up on a military research base, surrounded by brilliant engineers and physicists. In my family, smart people studied science, so when it came time to choose a career, I followed suit by studying environmental science at the University of California at Berkeley. In my first career out of college, I worked alongside and later managed scientists at the United States Environmental Protection Agency.

While I grew up with science and studied it formally, one thing never quite made sense: while the scientists who surrounded me prided themselves on being logical, their behavior was often anything but. After spending more than a decade as a scientific professional, I discovered that my true passion lay more in understanding the *human* operating system. To that end, I have immersed myself in studying advances in social neuroscience, experimental psychology, and evolutionary biology, and applying that information to help organizations become more productive, innovative, and collaborative.

The questions are endless: Why do we humans do what we do? Why, despite our belief that we're rational creatures, do we make so many irrational decisions? Why are we such slaves to bad habits and emotional triggers? Why can't we just "let it go?" My belief is that the more we understand our fundamental biological design and apply that insight into our personal lives and into the design of the organizations and communities in which we live, the more fulfilled and mature we'll be as individuals and the more productive and wise we'll become as groups.

## What Does Science Add to the Conversation?

Our culture has had a love affair with the rational brain, dating back nearly six hundred years to the scientific revolution. Science has accelerated our ability to manipulate our environment faster than any other tradition of inquiry or belief. As such, science is uniquely privileged by our society as the highest form of knowing.

Most people in our culture have an image of science as being the purview of the extremely smart: people in lab coats holding smoldering test tubes or physicists at a chalk board covered with complex mathematical formulas. The truth is that science is a systematic way of acquiring and testing knowledge— nothing more or less. Anyone who has a really good question or hypothesis, a well-formed experiment that attempts to prove...and disprove...that hypothesis, and a community of peers to review and challenge the results can be a scientist. In fact, one of the most profound results in neuroscience came from a simple, but elegant experimental set-up involving nothing more than a cardboard box and a mirror!

It is important to know that science is limited by our ability to construct an experiment and by the cultural mindsets we bring to the inquiry. Many phenomena remain too complex to be reduced, at least given the levels of scientific understanding to date. Often, we fail to ask questions in science because our cultural mindsets don't include a framework for "seeing" the phenomena that way. Also, because science *appears* to rely solely on conscious rational thought processes, the reduction of complex questions into individual component pieces, and the trust of the observable over the ephemeral, we have a tendency to dismiss anything that seems to call on the non-rational, intuitive, holistic and non-material worlds.

The resulting irony is that the very science that has been responsible for so many of our technological advancements also perpetuates a great many damaging myths about humanity. We treat emotions like unwanted stepchildren and our bodies as mere containers built to execute commands—nothing more than forms of locomotion that sometimes function well, but often break down. We believe that we are fundamentally selfish and that we operate in isolation as individuals. We act as if most of our behavior comes from conscious volition.

The beauty of recent social neuroscience research is that it is turning many Western beliefs about what it means to be human on their heads. We now know that the vast majority of our behavior and our decisions are determined before the thoughts hit our conscious minds. Instinct acquired from millions of years of evolution and a lifetime of learning stored in our subconscious mind guide us. At our core, we are social creatures, and a great deal of our neural circuitry is devoted to monitoring and assuring the health and safety of our social interactions. Our bodies and emotions have a rationality all their own, without which we cannot function, no matter how logical and intelligent we fancy ourselves to be. The conscious mind is like the very small percentage of an iceberg that sits above the waterline.

When we understand that hidden logic, we can gain huge insight, compassion and power to direct our lives and organizations more intentionally. Science is one window into wisdom, one pathway among many. Neuroscientific proof is hardly necessary for us to adopt new ways of being and to act in a more holistic and humane fashion. In a Western context, however, it's particularly helpful to use science to understand and break free of the limitations our belief systems have placed upon us.

For some readers, the science may provide the understanding necessary to suspend the suspicions raised by the Western business mindset. For others, it will simply enrich the material. I hope, in either case, that you leave with a fuller understanding and appreciation for the amazing biological design that is the human being.

## The Path

This part of *Leadership Embodiment* is organized into three sections:

In the first, we consider from a biological standpoint what produces our behavior: instinct, learned patterns, and conscious volition. We'll travel back in time to our tribal origins on the African Savannah in order to discover how our human instincts evolved. We'll look at how we acquire our individual personalities, emotional patterns and triggers. Finally, we'll examine the role of volition and the ability to consciously choose a path of action.

In the second, we look at how these three areas interrelate, particularly when we experience threat. What are the brain mechanisms at play during stress? What determines the mix of instinct, personality and volition in any given interaction? At a brain level, how much control do we have over behavior? How can we be more intentional about using our neural resources wisely?

Finally, we look at change and learning. Is it possible to change our personality and emotional patterns? What's the process for augmenting and/or shifting how we relate to them? How do the practices in this book function to transform our brain patterning?

My hope is that the content will be useful to you, the reader, in three ways:

- Understanding why the practices contained in this book work
- Providing a framework for (and confidence in) introducing the concepts to others who might not otherwise be open to them, and
- Giving you a new lens through which to observe the human "operating system," allowing you to discover new insight into the fascinating web of interactions around you.

# EIGHT

# Why We Do What We Do

### *The Three Legged Stool*

We seldom stop to consider why we do what we do throughout the day. While we have the sensation that we are consciously directing our lives, there's a bit of smoke and mirrors going on. The vast majority of our behavior is generated on autopilot, but because it happens outside of consciousness, we're not…well…conscious of it! Most neuroscientists would agree that 95-99+ percent of our behavior is the result of habits and instincts, along with other unconscious patterns that play themselves out in the background with little or no awareness on our part.

While we like to think of ourselves as "in control," it's a very good thing that we aren't most of the time. The brain has an extremely limited ability to process information real time, a capacity called "working memory." Were we to have to make original decisions about the myriad issues we face every moment of every day, the brain would be instantaneously overwhelmed.

Our behavior is generated in three ways:
- Instinctual patterns
- Learned patterns, and
- Volitional responses.

Instinctual responses are encoded in our DNA. We don't have to learn to feel uncomfortable standing at the edge of a great height. Our bodies come pre-equipped by millions of years of evolution to know that this is a precarious position. Likewise, we startle at any form resembling a snake. We didn't learn to do this. It came pre-loaded. At this level, all humans are more or less equal. Life experience can temper these instincts, making us more or less reactive, but the basic pattern is standard hardware.

Learned patterns are acquired from a lifetime of experience. As the brain seeks to successfully navigate the environment and social group into which an individual is born, it encodes patterns that make functional sense of its particular surroundings. At this level, individual humans vary tremendously, depending on the familial, social, geographic, and cultural realities they are faced with.

Volitional responses are generated primarily in an area of the brain called the prefrontal cortex, which sits just behind the forehead. Our biological ability to consciously guide our behavior is extremely limited, probably accounting for less than one percent of what we do. The brain tries to preserve this precious resource by relying as much as possible on pre-programmed patterns, both instinctual and learned.

We have a clever three part design of checks and balances: we come pre-equipped with the historically most important patterns for human survival, we learn new patterns based on the conditions of the particular group and point in history we are born into, and we can override both (albeit to a limited degree) if the real time conditions render instinct and learning insufficient to the demands of the present.

In modern times, we like to think of ourselves as being in control of our actions, when in reality, almost all of our behavior is dictated by evolutionary imprints and learned patterns. The illusion that we can change our behavior solely by thinking our way out of it is alluring, but biologically inaccurate. As we will see in future sections, the impulse to action occurs in the body before we ever have consciousness of it. By the time consciousness occurs, the pattern is already in full swing. By learning to catch and shift patterns while still at the stage of a somatic marker, we can circumvent the cascade of triggers that lead to less desirable behaviors.

Most training addresses the conscious mind. With our cultural belief that logic calls the shots, we think that understanding what needs to change and why is enough. In other words, we focus on using one percent of the brain's behavioral drivers to attempt to control the ninety-nine percent that's causing most of the behavior. We quickly learn that understanding alone leads only to understanding. What we really want to accomplish is a change in what we *do* and the *effect we have* on others. Our willpower and conscious minds are no match for the vast storehouse of programming that they are up against. We have to learn to relate to our unconscious programming differently, and this is where Leadership Embodiment shines.

## Leg One: Instinct

### *How Evolution Shaped Our Brains*

On the timescale of human biology, modernity represents an eye blink. Our species and forbearers have been on the planet roughly four million years, yet almost all the significant advances that we associate with our modern lifestyles developed only in the last ten thousand years. Things like agriculture, permanent settlements, domestication of animals, and written language are newcomers to our existence when viewed on an evolutionary scale.

To look at this another way, were we to reduce our species' evolution to the span of one year, we left the African Savannah a mere four to five days ago. The first civilizations developed less than a day ago. The scientific revolution clocks in at roughly one hour ago, and the digital revolution in which we're all living represents a few eye blinks.

Over the course of our evolutionary history, the way humans live has undergone many seismic shifts. Agriculture allowed us to leave our nomadic lifestyles and reside in small permanent settlements. As our agricultural savvy grew, an increasingly smaller segment of the population was needed for the production of food, freeing large numbers to pursue specialized trades. Written language allowed us to codify and transmit learning across generations and from one to many. The printing press enabled mass distribution of knowledge that theretofore had been restricted to a small elite learned class. The scientific and industrial revolutions gave us enormous power to manipulate the natural world and enabled mass production of inexpensive consumer goods.

Humans have an almost magical prefrontal capability to imagine new futures and through language, to coordinate action with other humans to bring that vision to fruition. Those futures, or as we call them, "innovations," usually center on strategies to make our existence safer, easier and more pleasurable. For example, agriculture freed us from relying on the natural environment for sustenance and from the need to follow the food. The irony is that each time we innovate to make life easier, we also move ourselves further and further into lifestyles that are out of sync with our biological design.

Our brains and cultures do evolve to adapt to changes in the human condition, but those adaptations happen slowly. We've reached a point where the pace of our innovation has far outstripped the pace of evolutionary adaptation. The vast majority of our instinctual programming developed in response to conditions present throughout the millions of years of pre-modernity. These hidden patterns still leave us extremely sensitive to anything that might have been a threat back then. At the same time, we are remarkably vulnerable to new threats to which we haven't yet evolved a sufficient instinctual recognition.

## Life on the Savannah

What, exactly, were those early conditions under which we spent the lion's share of our evolutionary history? Humans lived in small nomadic tribes of a few hundred members. You were born into a tribe and likely remained there your entire life. The exception was leaving to join another tribe through intermarriage, an act requiring elaborate rituals to transact.

Pause for a moment and imagine yourself in a meeting space containing ten rows of chairs with twenty chairs each. Now imagine that each chair is occupied with a person whom you've known most of your life. You've spent hours every day in their company, you know their entire life history, and you rely upon them intimately for your survival. Now imagine that you rarely interact with anyone outside this group. For the vast majority of our history as a species, that was reality.

Racial diversity was non-existent. Strangers were few, far between, and not to be trusted. The constraints of living in a 100 percent natural environment ensured that your food was organic, free range, and unprocessed. The daily demands of a nomadic lifestyle, coupled with the exercise incumbent with procuring food, meant that your body was fit and toned. We enjoyed unlimited fresh air and sunlight, and ample downtime to enjoy the close intimate company of the tribespeople with whom we'd spent our entire lives.

Under those early primitive conditions, what do you suppose was the biggest threat to survival? For most of us, starvation pops up as the immediate response, but we'd be wrong. Food was relatively plentiful on the Savannah, and there weren't a lot of humans competing for it yet. You *did* have to work hard to gather and hunt your food. To do so effectively required collaboration with others. Humans are wimpy creatures compared with most other mammals on the Savannah. Our upright two-legged form of locomotion makes us slower, less nimble, and less powerful than the other predators with whom we cohabitated. Our advantage was our intelligence and our ability to collaborate in groups. A lone human on the Savannah quickly becomes dinner.

Quite simply, we evolved to rely on each other. In contrast to the modern Western belief that we operate individually, motivated purely by self-interest, neuroscience is showing that we're biologically built to be exquisitely aware of others and to care deeply about what they think. As such, a large proportion of our neural resources are devoted to attending to our social environment, so much so that in the absence of anything more salient to pay attention to, this is the brain's default position. Because this network operates mostly outside of consciousness, it's easy to turn a blind eye to the effect it has on our decisions and behavior, especially when our cultural beliefs encourage us to do so. But, as U.C.L.A. Professor of Neuroscience, Matthew Lieberman, put it, "Evolution made a bet that the best use of your brain when it isn't doing something else specific is to use its extra processing resources to think about the social world, other people, and yourself."

## Social Awareness

In 1992, neuroscience researchers in Parma, Italy made an accidental, but revolutionary discovery. While studying motor movement in Macau monkeys, a researcher reached for a banana. To his surprise, the brain regions responsible for the same movement lit up in the monkey being scanned. Ironically, the discovery was initially sent to *Nature*, but was rejected for its "lack of general interest." Despite that initial dismissal, this finding ultimately led to one of the most exciting recent discoveries in neuroscience: specialized neurons known as "mirror neurons" which map the physiology of others in our social field.

While the study of mirror neurons in humans is still in the early stages, it appears that we, too, come equipped with specialized neurons that allow us to map the physiology of other humans in our midst. It happens outside of consciousness and informs every relationship we have. We don't often consciously think about the degree of tension around someone's eyes, how deeply they breathe, or the stiffness or fluidity with which they walk. When someone enters into our physical space of awareness, however, this unconscious mapping system is likely helping to determine how we feel about them: whether we trust them, feel threatened, ignored, or accepted.

It's easy to spot the effect of our social awareness circuits in action. Humans have an innate ability to sense the emotional state of those around us and to empathically mirror it at an unconscious level. Think of a time when you witnessed someone injure himself. You likely winced in empathy and may even have had a physical sensation like localized tingling or a reflexive urge to cover that part of your anatomy. The phenomenon shows up in our language as well. We witness someone stumbling through a public talk, inwardly cringe, and say that it was "painful" to watch.

## Nonverbal Signals

Understanding the internal emotional state of others is central to our ability to function in social groups. Humans have what neuroscientists call "theory of mind." Stated simply, this means we are able to decode a huge range of verbal and nonverbal signals to assess the intent and internal state of the other humans with whom we interact. The vast majority of what we communicate about our state is implicit. It is sent and received without the conscious brain's involvement.

Much of this information is transmitted through our nonverbal body positioning. It seems that certain gestures and postures have universal meaning among humans. A dignified upright and relaxed posture indicates confidence, status and power. A collapsed chest and slumped shoulders indicate depression, defeat and subordinance. Gestures made with palms facing up indicate requests for help and lack of threat. Gestures with palms down most often indicate certainty and control.

Science is beginning to map these gestures and to trace the effect they have on the physiology of the displayer and those witnessing the display. What's clear is that there is an intimate interplay between gesture and neurotransmitters, the chemicals that determine our emotional states. It's not an accident that we feel more powerful when we stand tall. In very short order, that stance increases our testosterone levels, equating with higher confidence.[1]

The gestures I've mentioned here are at a gross level, but we're just as sensitive to micro patterns: twitches, eye tension, skin color, breathing patterns, etc. Usually, we can't consciously identify the nonverbal patterns that lead to our emotional assessment of others, but the unconscious mind is processing them in every interaction we have.

What Leadership Embodiment trains is a heightened awareness of one's own body state, distinctions around which body dispositions are productive in which circumstances, and the ability to catch oneself and correct quickly when we go into unproductive states.

## Congruence

Our bodies and brains are built for congruence. It requires quite a bit of cognitive effort to maintain a physical stance that is incongruent with our thoughts and intentions. Try this out yourself: Adopt the body stance of depression and try to talk extemporaneously about how confident and self-assured you feel. It's not easy. Now try it in a congruent posture and note the difference.

When we expend energy to cover up parts of ourselves, it's likely that the incongruence is leaking out in our nonverbal behavior anyway. Champion poker players are famous for their ability to detect even the most subtle physical cues, known in the trade as "tells." I've worked with many high level leaders who are very accomplished, but always in a "prove myself" mode. Invariably, when I conduct feedback interviews with their colleagues, they make comments about how they wish the leader would stop trying to prove how confident and smart they are, or that the leader would be more accessible if they would show a few cracks in their façade.

It's not uncommon for people to have a low level of awareness of the internal conversation and set of beliefs that are driving their physical expression. Again, instinct and learned habits inform the majority of who we are and what we do. Often, it's not until we see ourselves in video or get feedback from others that we become cognizant of the message we are sending and the thoughts that are driving it.

Congruence is a byproduct of our neural architecture. The brain has about a one hundred billion neurons that are joined together into networks that encode our thoughts, habits, memories, etc. Each neuron is part of multiple networks, only one of which can be activated at any given time. The brain attempts to organize the networks with a coherency such that out of all the millions of possibilities, related information is rapidly accessi-

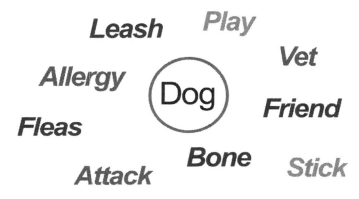

**8a-** Priming

ble. When you think "dog," your brain warms its circuitry so that concepts like "leash" or "man's best friend" can be easily retrieved. This phenomenon is called priming. It not only makes context appropriate retrieval easier, but it blocks retrieval of incongruent data.

It's important to note that body state is a far more powerful influencer of congruence than intellectual expression. When we hold our body in a way that's congruent with expansiveness and ease, the memories, abilities, and attitudes of openness and ease come to bear on the situation being considered. Conversely, when we verbally espouse openness and ease, but do so from the body disposition of irritation, the congruent memories of difficulty, frustration, and upset become readily available. The networks and neurotransmitters associated with that posture create a tsunami of conflicting signals, both to our self and to others.

Because social cohesion was so critically important to survival back on the Savannah, evolution has made us extremely good at detecting incongruence. We may not be able to explicitly pinpoint the basis of our feelings, but when others aren't 100 percent behind what they are saying, our unconscious brain produces a sense of unease and distrust. When you are "unified," i.e. your body posture matches what you are saying, you are believable. When not, you send the classic mixed message.

### Social Instincts

We all know what instinct looks like in other animals. Dangle a string in front of a kitten and watch the adorable and quite predictable response. Human attention will be instantaneously diverted by any sharp noise, flash of light, or quick movement. All of these were physical signals on the Savannah of a predator or potential prey. We respond to them still, even when it's just your email counter bouncing up and down or your cell phone letting you know you've received a text message.

While we don't usually think of instincts as impacting our *social* interactions, survival has embedded instinctual responses to social stimuli into our essential make up. Human beings come preloaded with a variety of social needs, things like status, inclusion, relatedness, and predictability. We have a tendency to think that these sensitivities are the outcome of individual personality or ego, but the reality is that they are shared by us all. When these needs are threatened or we relate to them in unskilled and unmindful ways, it impacts our ability to think intelligently and creatively.

## Status

All social animals have status hierarchies, and our brains are built to be exceedingly sensitive to status violations. On the Savannah, our standing in the tribe mattered...a lot! Those with high status were likely to get the choicest food, most protection, and largest selection of potential mates. For those with low status, life could be precarious.

We signal our status in almost every aspect of what we do. The external indicators, like what car we drive or what school we went to or the size of our family, vary depending on your group affiliations. In contrast, nonverbal signals, the most fundamental indicators of power and status, are more universal. Not only does our posture communicate to others how to assess our status, it communicates it to our self.

It's popular in democratic societies to eschew status, as if drawing these distinctions makes us somehow less evolved. For the most part, all this does is to drive status underground, where it occasionally shows up in ironically comical manifestations. Lack of concern about status, after all, makes one better than all the people who seek it!

Status generally operates in the background, causing us to make moves in an attempt to manage our standing. Our justification, even internally, is almost never, "I disagreed because I didn't want him to look good in front of the group." Our conscious brains are wickedly clever at generating politically correct rationalizations that appear dispassionate and logically sound. Unfortunately, when we're stressed, we tend to relate to status as a zero sum game, unknowingly operating from a presupposition that granting status to others will lower our own.

Two patterns commonly emerge. In the first, we engage in power grabs. We indulge in behaviors like name-dropping.

We fail to include others on email communications. We make sure our contributions are highlighted. Conversely, if we feel that our status is low relative to others, we may shrink and withdraw in order to avoid the danger of affronting someone with more power.

Leaders acting out of base instinct often unconsciously try to improve their status by lowering the status of those around them. This can happen in a multitude of ways: talking over another person in a meeting, recognizing certain people over others, even such subtle cues as whom he or she makes eye contact with and whose gaze is avoided. In the name of efficiency, leaders may take away agency through micromanagement or leave stakeholders off meeting invites with no explanation. The net result is a team operating under social threat, with, as we will soon see, an accompanying diversion of cognitive resources.

The key is not to deny the existence of this primal drive, but to manage it consciously to enhance the communities that we live and work in. When we grab status with knee jerk reflexivity, we create an environment of threat throughout the groups with whom we interact. There are many ways to increase the status of those around us without lowering our own. Listening to and acknowledging ideas, praising accomplishments, and noticing unique skills all boost status. More universally, adopting the mindset and body disposition of "we are in this together" sends the message that everyone matters and belongs. Leaders who relate to status consciously have the power to create environments where everyone can win.

## Inclusion

Whether or not we're included is the most basic indicator of the strength of our social affiliation. For our tribal ancestors, exclusion meant almost certain death. To this day, we are exquisitely sensitive to the myriad cues that tell us where we stand in relation to the others in our social group. The Western culture of independence tells us we should be self-determined and immune to the opinions of others, so we often pretend it doesn't matter. In truth, we are designed to care, so much so that exclusion is processed in the same brain centers that process the distress of physical pain. Our language is full of expressions equating emotional and physical distress (hurt feelings, broken hearted, sore loser, bruised ego). It turns out that the connection is more than metaphorical.

A 2003 U.C.L.A. study by Naomi Eisenberger et al. elegantly proves the point.[2] In it, participants submitted to fMRI scanning while playing a simple computer game of ball tossing with two other virtual players. Unbeknownst to the subject being studied, the other players don't exist in reality, but are instead, a computer algorithm. Once the subject develops a comfortable rhythm of ball tossing, the two other "players" exclude him, tossing the ball back and forth only amongst themselves. Not only did the anterior cingulate cortex, the area responsible for processing physical pain, show heightened activity, the participants reported experiencing extreme emotional discomfort during the trial. As Dr. Eisenberger says, "we would never tell someone to 'get over' having a broken leg, yet we'll say the same for a broken heart."

## Relatedness vs. Difference

A third instinctual category is perceived difference. On the Savannah, we knew the other humans in our tribe intimately. They came from exactly the same racial, ethnic, cultural and familial background as we did. Together, we played, danced, hunted, cooked, told stories, napped, and cared for children. Day in and day out, we engaged in all of life's activities with the same group of people. They were like us in general, and we had participated in their entire life history as individuals. We knew how they were likely to respond under any given circumstance, and we had a long history of interdependence in the provision of our most basis needs. They were trustable.

Contrast that with a stranger from a different tribe. We don't know the customs, the personalities, the quirks. We have no track record with them, and we have little basis for assessing whether our needs and goals align. The less familiar (even the word proves the concept) someone is, the less we can predict their behavior, the less basis for trust we have, and the more dangerous they become.

A large body of neuroscience research deals with the subject of "in group" and "out group" behavior. The results are consistent. At a neural level, we process those in our in group in markedly more prosocial ways. Studies of implicit bias have shown that people are very often unaware of their own internal biases. Consciously, they believe in acceptance and inclusion, but at a neural level, they still process those who are different through a stereotyped lens. In the extreme, those whom we code as very different fail to activate the areas of our brain devoted to processing human life forms.

The insidious outgrowth of our evolutionary legacy is that we often neurally code difference as danger, when in fact, it is only difference. When we meet someone who acts or looks different from what we are accustomed to, our biology tells us to distrust them until we have more information. This is at the root of much discriminatory behavior. It isn't so much a character flaw or moral failing as it is our unconscious biological programming in motion.

In today's world, this neural design poses a huge challenge. Cognitively, we may espouse egalitarian and inclusive workplaces and communities, but our actions often arise from unconscious instinctual programming. Subtle and not so subtle exclusion based on difference happens all the time, often without the excluder ever knowing that he or she is doing it. It happens at the level of whom we choose to form workplace friendships with, whom we promote, whom we initiate conversation with, and whom we ask for advice.

Several years ago, I was a keynote speaker for a leadership conference at a Fortune 100 technology company and had been invited to sit with the top leadership at a kickoff dinner. Half the table where I was seated was from the United States and the other half hailed from various Asian countries. Partway through the dinner, I realized that I'd only been conversing with the Americans. I couldn't say why, except that I just felt more comfortable talking with them. If we're honest and pay attention, we recognize that we all carry this tendency. The beauty is that if we can recognize it, name it, and move to inclusion, we build familiarity and inclusivity while modeling it for those who follow our lead.

The fact that it's biology doesn't let us off the hook. Mature, high-functioning adults can monitor their reactions and adopt strategies to overcome instinctual bias against those who are different. In part, we do this naturally. You may have observed that people who are deeply engaged in positive conversation with each other start sitting and moving alike. They may cross and uncross their legs in quick succession or reach for their coffee at the same moment. Even such unconscious actions as breathing may start to align. At its best, this physiological mirroring creates similarity, calming the brain's threat centers and allowing both parties to relax into their highest thinking capabilities.

Familiarity can trump difference, and we can create this consciously at both the micro and the macro levels. The more favorable experience we have with other cultures, ethnicities, and social classes, the less of a threat they become. They are still different, but they are no longer as unfamiliar and unpredictable. We may gain this knowledge as a natural outgrowth of our life experiences, but the more we consciously cultivate interactions that augment and enrich our library, the more open and flexible we become. We are able to interact positively with a broad range of people, and in turn, can build rich networks of trust. To do so, however, requires that we be able to manage our natural tendency to shut down in the face of difference.

The consequences of whether we choose to develop in this area are real and not trivial. Innovation relies on diversity, and never before has the world been in such dire need of prosocial creativity to solve the global problems that confront us. Overcoming our innate biological tendency to distrust difference necessitates awareness and practice. Leadership Embodiment teaches the body to relax and welcome, while remaining grounded, principled and strong. By doing the practices, we train our awareness and create the body and mental priming for openness and inclusivity.

## Conformity

Related to our need for inclusion and our distrust of difference is an innate tendency to unconsciously conform to the behavioral standards of the groups to which we belong. Again, most of us in Western society like to think we're charting our own paths as individuals, but the truth is that very little of what we do is the result of individual measured decisions.

As an example, think about trends. In the 1970s, avocado green, orange, and mustard yellow appliances were all the rage. If you had a stylish and modern kitchen, chances were that it followed this color scheme. Now, unless your identity centers on being retro (in which case you probably flock together with other hip retro friends), we find these interiors hideously tacky. Everything, from trends in clothing, décor, and technology, to our standards for beauty and acceptable behavior, changes as the flock adapts to find a common norm. Even in notoriously counter cultural environments like the famous social experiment turned party-in-the-desert known as Burning Man, you'll see an amazing similarity in style of dress among the artistically "self-expressed" participants!

Research spearheaded by Jamil Zaki, Jessica Schirmer, and Jason Mitchell at Harvard University shows that we are biologically designed to conform to the norms and perceptions of the societal groups to which we belong. We think we're making up our own minds, drawing on our unique perspective and values. Despite this explicit belief, it's quite easy to get people to change their preferences without their ever knowing they've been influenced.

In one experiment, male subjects were shown 180 digitized photos of women and asked to rate their attractiveness on a scale of one to seven. The participants were told that hundreds of their peers had also rated the faces. After assigning each score, participants saw their own rating displayed for two seconds and then saw the *supposed* average ranking of their peers for an additional two seconds. Unbeknownst to the participants, the ratings were computer generated to artificially raise the scores for some of the less attractive individuals and lower the scores for some of the more attractive individuals. After thirty minutes had passed, the participants re-rated the photos. While subjects felt that viewing peer rankings had not influenced them, the evidence showed otherwise. Previously unattractive faces were ranked as more beautiful, while formerly lovely faces held less attraction. Furthermore, brain scans showed that the re-evaluation happened at a neural level. The subjects weren't simply going along to fit in with their peers: they'd internally adopted the standards of the group.[3]

While this biological tendency may seem horrifying at first, it has huge survival value. Imagine a world where all of us battled constantly to reconcile each and every personal preference with those of others. What would it be like to live in a world where there were no generally agreed upon social norms? We don't see all the ways that conformity and our biologically driven social web serve to create peace, harmony and productivity. The key for leadership is to be able to recognize when the shadow side of this biological tendency is blocking new and useful ideas, preventing intervention against harmful situations, or causing us to adopt norms that lack sustainable wisdom.

We've all experienced the dark side of social conformity. If you're honest, you can probably recall an instance where you went along with the behavior of the group, but later felt guilt or even self recrimination for not doing what you *should* have done.

This common experience accounts for the universal appeal of television programs like "Candid Camera" and "What Would You Do?" We get to vicariously witness a situation that's clearly unacceptable, but where no one is reacting to the scene. There's a moment of indecision. Does the television dupe trust their gut or do they trust the evaluation of the group? We watch and would like to think that were we in the situation, we'd do the right thing, but we never know until we're confronted with the decision in reality.

To this point, you will never see a television show whose premise is to show people going along with the group when that's a neutral or morally good decision. We do that more often than not, but there's no dramatic and universally relevant dilemma or horrifying display of human frailty. It wouldn't make for interesting television or useful learning.

Wisdom is in knowing when to conform and when to act apart from the tribe. It is having the discernment to notice when taking a stand is called for and the ability to do so with dignity and strength. In Leadership Embodiment, we practice an awareness of our own space and our ground. We cultivate the ability to stand strongly in our principles while also remaining open, curious and inclusive to the group. By doing so, we can adapt when conforming serves the harmony of the group, and we can stand apart when the group is mindlessly conforming to a standard that conflicts with what we believe will serve higher principles.

### *Group Intelligence*

Another indicator that we may have gotten it wrong with our emphasis on individual achievement and intellectual prowess is recent research on group intelligence. Our schools and to a large extent, workplaces, place emphasis on individual achievement and competition, believing that the way to bring out the best is through encouraging each individual to win over all the rest. The inevitable result is that some group members thrive, while others fall to the bottom of the status ladder, and, as we will see in the next section, may suffer stunted cognitive performance as a result.

If I haven't drilled it in by now, we are built to live in groups and our brain design is social. Up until recently, research on intelligence focused on the individual. In 2010, scientists at MIT and Carnegie Mellon created a measure for the intelligence of groups and then looked for correlating data to account for differences in scores.[4] What they found surprised many in the academic and corporate world. Group intelligence was not dependent on the average or maximum individual IQs of group members. High group intelligence scores, however, did correlate to three factors:

- The average social sensitivity of group members,
- The equality in distribution of conversational turn-taking, and
- The proportion of females in the group.

It is precisely the dispositions of inclusiveness, curiosity, and openness taught by Leadership Embodiment that enhance the ability to act intelligently as a collective.

### Stress

A final area related to our evolutionary history is stress. Recently, stress has gotten a very bad reputation. It underlies everything from belly fat, heart attacks and alcoholism, to depression, memory impairment and chronic underperformance. For most of our evolutionary history, however, stress has been more friend than foe. When we encounter a potential threat, the stress reaction prepares the body to rapidly handle the situation. Cortisol and adrenaline course through our system. Blood flow is diverted away from digestion, tissue repair and reproduction. It's all hands on deck to help us overcome an imminent threat and live to see another day.

Our biology is primarily designed to manage episodic and rapid physical threat. Were you to encounter a predator on the plains of Africa, the ensuing scenarios were limited: you outran it, fought it off, or made yourself still enough to escape detection. In any case, the threat was sudden and it resolved itself in your favor…or not…on short order. Both running and fighting served to clear stress hormones out of your physical system. When the threat was over, it truly was over.

Fast forward to today. Our evolutionary coding tells us to react to stressors in the modern world that no longer represent threats to our survival. In the past, a flash of light, sudden movement, or a sharp noise like a twig breaking were all indicators of a predator and warranted our full attention and quick response. Now, we startle when a computer icon bounces or our myriad technology gadgets vibrate or ring. The environment is full, often to the point of sensory overload, with unexpected noises, lights, and movement, yet rarely do they indicate anything truly dangerous.

Social threat cues also abound. Our daily worlds are filled with strangers, unpredictable outcomes, and uncertain status. Running away, freezing, or fighting rarely constitutes a useful and appropriate response. When the "predator" is someone across the table in the boardroom who has just attacked our favorite project, we don't (hopefully!) hit them or run to a hiding place. We still experience the physiological stress response, but the outward manifestation is a psychological equivalent:

we clam up, say something sarcastic, shut down and check our email, or forget our presentation.

The powerful hormones released to prepare us for gross muscular movement now have no way to exit the system. Instead, they circulate, damaging the body and leaving us primed to be even more easily triggered. Instead of the episodic threats we're designed to handle, we now face continual change and non-stop pressure. Modern life exposes us to an ongoing barrage of false threat cues. Unacknowledged and unmanaged, the cumulative effect is life in a soup of stress chemicals never meant to persist beyond their momentary utility.

To make matters worse, for most of our history it has been beneficial to overreact to threats rather than under-react. Better to be intently alert to rustling in the grass than to ignore it. If you fail to detect a tiger or snake, you risk death. If you activate your muscles for flight and it's only a bird, no harm done. In either case, on the Savannah, your default lifestyle (lots of walking, sunlight, social connection, etc.) ensured that stress hormones processed through and out of your system quickly.

These automatic responses no longer serve us in the way they were evolutionarily designed. The practice of Centering is the practice of wresting control back from these instinctive responses, so that instead of responding reflexively from habit or fight and flight, we are engaging with the stressor from a place of curiosity and calm.

Now that we've considered the first level of behavior generation, instinct, let's turn our attention to the second level, learned responses.

## Leg Two: Learned Responses

Unlike many other animals, humans don't rely primarily on instinct to guide our behavior. Our species has an enormous capacity to learn and to adapt to the circumstances of the present. Human lifestyle and preferences vary tremendously from culture to culture and over time. How do we end up with the thoughts, beliefs, habits and motivations that guide our lives?

### *The Brain as a Pattern Making Organ*

A useful metaphor for the brain is a massive pattern detection and encoding machine. If you stop to think about the world surrounding you, you'll quickly realize that there is far more data "out there" than you can possibly notice and make sense of. The brain's job is to figure out which aspects of our environment are essential to our ability to function well and to categorize them into complex networks of neural patterns that allow us to know how to respond as we encounter each new situation we face throughout the day.

To make sense of this, consider a simple example: getting dressed in the morning. As basic as this is, it's an incredibly complex activity. Recall what it's like for a young child as they transition to dressing themselves. They are likely to pick out inappropriate clothing, put their shoes on the wrong feet, fail to consider the weather in their choices, and not be bothered by the large grape juice stain in the middle of their t-shirt. A really young child might simply leave the house naked, having not yet adopted their culture's pattern for modesty!

As an adult getting ready for the day, you flip through a vast unconscious file of information. You automatically think ahead to the types of situations you'll face and adjust your clothing choices to fit the context. If your day holds business meetings, but you always meet your workout partner for a lunchtime run on Wednesdays, you pack your running clothes. You don't have to think about what to wear for running — you just know. Your shoes go on the right feet without a moment's consideration, and you probably have a particular order in which you put your clothing items on.

Just getting dressed for the day involves hundreds of choices, but your conscious brain makes very few of them. Those choices were made long ago and encoded into neural patterns. Once encoded, all your brain needs to do is hit the "play button" for the right neural pattern, and its job is done. While we go through the process of getting ready for the day, our minds are largely occupied with thoughts completely unrelated to getting dressed.

The in-the-moment ability to process information and make decisions is an extremely limited neural resource — one that the brain seeks to reserve for situations requiring a novel response. Because of this, the brain attempts to create templates or patterns that can automatically respond to the conditions we face. Those patterns tell us both what to notice and how to respond.

An interior decorator notices different data about the environment than a meteorologist. Both might be sitting in the same room, but one notices the color of the paint and how it compliments the texture in the carpet, while the other stares out the window and speculates on the probability of rain given the cloud formations and wind patterns. Both individuals have contextual access to the same data, but their neural patterns will determine what data they actually notice. They are blind to that which isn't relevant to the life they've chosen.

As with instinct, learned patterns operate outside of consciousness. The interior architect doesn't consciously decide to notice the color of the rug, it just happens. The adult who was abandoned as an infant doesn't choose to be overly sensitive to signs that her partner might leave, the pattern is seared into her neural makeup.

### Emotional Patterns

Just like we have patterns for the material objects we notice and the societal rules that we conform to, we also have patterns that govern our relational and emotional lives. When functional, these patterns serve to organize the world into something that has meaning and help us to navigate our relationships successfully. When the patterns form under dysfunctional or outmoded circumstances, however, they can lead us powerfully astray.

Our survival and success depend in large part on learning from past experience in an attempt to minimize threat and maximize reward in the future. Emotional learning involves the encoding of sensitive neural patterns which develop in response to repeated relational interactions and observations. These patterns sit ready to spring into action, shaping our perception of threat and opportunity in our current relationships. Whenever we sense something in the present with enough similarity to a past emotionally salient memory, the accompanying neural response pattern is triggered. At lightning speed and outside of conscious awareness, we interpret the current situation through the lens of that past experience.

Usually, this is a highly effective way to navigate our environment and relationships. Were it not for this phenomenon, we'd have to relearn how to relate to people every time we encountered them. The problem, however, comes when the associations we have with a stimulus no longer serve us. Not only are old memories pulled up, but those memories prime us to notice congruent information in the here and now, reinforcing the pattern and creating a self fulfilling prophesy.

Have you ever noticed how several people can sit in the same meeting and have very different emotional stories about what happened? Some will view a behavior as humorous, while another will label it as obnoxious. One will see it as a legitimate professional response, while another will interpret it as a personal attack. The response of each individual in the room has more to do with his or her past experience and stored neural patterns than it does with the intent of the behavior of the observed party.

### How "Personality" Develops

Humans are one of the most helpless of all species at birth, and we remain almost fully dependent on grown adults for over a decade. The human brain continues to develop well into the teenage years. In males, in fact, it does not reach full maturity until the early twenties.

At birth, our autonomic nervous system is incapable of self-regulation. We are born with what is referred to as "open neurology." Even stabilization of such basic bodily functions as respiration and heartbeat depend on physical contact with the nervous systems of those who care for us. Babies who are fed and changed, but do not receive adequate touch will die. At that age, touch is nearly as crucial to their survival as food and water. Through contact with an adult human, the nervous system learns how to regulate its own heart rhythm, temperature, breathing, etc.

When faced with danger or pain, we likewise do not innately know how to interpret the seriousness of the signals. In order to learn how to respond to the world around us, our bodies mimic the reactions of those most closely bonded to us.

It is at this early stage of development that our most sensitive emotional patterns are encoded.

Our personality is the result of a complex mix of genetic tendencies along with the influence of these early parental and societal imprints. As infants, we are helpless. Our tiny bodies depend completely on our parental caregivers for survival. The only evidence necessary to prove that the patterns of our parents are functional is that they survived long enough to produce us. As a result, we acquire patterning indiscriminately. If our parent was alcoholic, highly stressed, or angry at the opposite sex, our bodies still pick up these patterns as key to our survival.

Later in life, we may cognitively recognize that a particular emotional trigger doesn't serve us, but our conscious override system is usually no match for the deeply embedded, albeit erroneous, biological connection our brain makes between the pattern and our survival.

Our basic personality patterns are developed in early childhood, many before the age of two or three. At this age, the part of the brain responsible for autobiographical memory, the hippocampus, is not yet fully on line, nor is the seat of reason, the prefrontal cortex. We have no conscious memory of how we acquired the beliefs that shape our interpretation of the world, nor did we have a way to rationally examine their validity at the time of acquisition. Because of this, our reactions can feel like the only natural response rather than one of many possible ways of experiencing a situation.

Since these early patterns are acquired through somatic learning, they live first in our bodies. They reside outside consciousness until something has us observe and make distinctions about them. The patterns that shape our reactions fire automatically. The brain processes environmental input and selects an appropriate response before the conscious mind engages. Our rational brain has very limited override capability and often fails to catch that we are in the grip of an unskillful response until it's far too late to avoid damage.

Our reactions manifest first in the body as a felt sense or somatic shape. In Leadership Embodiment, we practice recognizing and transforming that shape without having to engage the relatively slow and limited powers of the rational mind. By engaging with our particular triggers at the somatic level, we can retrain our relationship to our personality patterns, learning to recognize and shift to a more resourceful somatic pattern quickly.

## Leg Three: Conscious Volition

We've examined two of the three legs of the behavioral stool: instinct and learned patterns. Both these levels operate outside our conscious awareness, yet they are responsible for the lion's share of our day-to-day behavior. But we humans are different. We have free will. We can consciously navigate our lives, resist impulses, and steer toward our goals…or can we?

It's true and it's not. Western Civilization has had a several hundred-year love affair with rationality and the functions of the so-called higher brain. We have a belief that we call the shots. We're captains of our destiny and the architects of our lives, but the reality is far more complex. We do have the ability to override instinct and learned patterns, but as a neural resource, that capacity is extremely limited. We live lifestyles and engage in practices that rob us of this limited resource and then expect it to work overtime. We think it's personal weakness when it fails us.

### *What is the Higher Brain?*

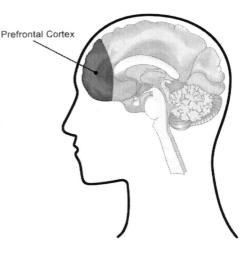

Prefrontal Cortex

**8b-** The Prefrontal Cortex

The human brain consists of many highly networked areas and structures. While we rely on every part of our brain in order to function, certain areas are crucial to the behaviors that we judge to be most highly evolved. The prefrontal cortex, the region just behind your forehead, is central to an impressive array of such behaviors, including emotional balance, the regulation of bodily systems, attuned communication, intuition, strategic thought, fear moderation, response flexibility (the ability to override an impulse), empathy and morality.[5] It is integral to volitional information processing: memorizing, recollection, and generating new insight.

When the prefrontal cortex (PFC) is functioning well, we have the ability to enter into stressful situations with grace, feeling the tug of our more instinctual responses, but not being bound to succumb to them. We use it, when necessary, to override our deeper habitual or instinctual drives. The PFC activates the release of a calming neurochemical called GABA (gamma amino butyric acid) that inhibits the automatic triggering process.

Despite its superpower capacities, the PFC has extremely limited bandwidth and is highly sensitive to how safe or threatening the environment is. As Yale University Professor Amy

Arnsten puts it, "The prefrontal cortex is the Goldilocks of the brain. In order to function well, it wants everything just right!"

Self-care, as in exercise, sunlight, healthy natural diet, and sleep, all significantly enhance the functioning of the PFC. Consistent with our social design, so does healthy social connection. Recent research suggests that altruism exerts a similarly positive effect. A robust research literature demonstrates that mindfulness and centering practices also have the power to strengthen this part of the brain.

The implications are two-fold. The PFC is no match for the cumulative strength of our emotional patterns. We cannot rely solely on a conscious rational approach to modify our most fundamental triggers and personality patterns. We expend huge amounts of neural effort in order to do so, and the amount of neural capacity available to us is likely insufficient to the task. Second, the PFC gets involved late in the game. Our patterned responses have already decided on a course of action by the time we're consciously aware of an impulse. The PFC has an extremely narrow window to catch and inhibit the response and is most often consumed with other competing tasks.

Leadership Embodiment practices help on two levels. First, they are a form of mindfulness practice and thus likely enhance the neural bandwidth of the higher brain and its inhibitory capabilities. Second, and more importantly, the redirection of behavioral response is already happening at the somatic level before impulses surface to a level necessitating cortical intervention.

## *A Quick Review*

1. **The Western model of the rational man is being shaken by recent neuroscience discoveries.**

   • Most behavior is not volitional.

   • The rational mind plays a limited role in producing behavior.

   • The body plays a far greater role than we've previously thought in the production of our reality.

2. **Behavior** is generated in three ways:

   • Instinct

   • Learned Patterns

   • Volitional Control

3. **Instinctual behavior** is shaped by our evolutionary past on the African Savannah.

   • We are designed to be social animals and a high proportion of our brain circuitry is devoted to sensing the emotional state of others.

   • Much of the information we transmit and receive about our state is nonverbal and most of the processing is outside consciousness.

   • Our social design makes us inherently sensitive to indicators of status, inclusion, and relatedness, and it drives us to conform to social norms without knowing we're doing so.

   • The same design may account for group intelligence being related to the social and interactional skills of group members.

- The stress reactions that protected us under the primitive conditions on the Savannah often no longer serve to enhance our survival.

4. **Learned Patterns** are acquired throughout our lives and are dependent on our individual life history and the environment to which we've been exposed.

    - The brain has limited capacity to process information real time and tries to automate our response to the environment as much as possible.

    - The brain is a meaning making and pattern recognition machine. It looks for meaningful relationships between objects and events in the external world and seeks to organize these into useful maps for how we should respond in the future.

    - The most fundamental maps, our emotional personalities, form very early in life before we have the ability to make conscious memories. They seem like the only possible reality because we have no memory of how we acquired them.

    - We each have individual personality patterns which inform how we respond to the circumstances of the here and now.

    - Our patterns can also constrict what we see in the environment.

    - These emotional reaction patterns reside first in the body as somatic patterns or bodily shapes. Reshaping and realigning these patterns is best done at this level.

5. **Conscious Volition** constitutes a slender layer atop a vast sea of unconscious behavior generators.

- The prefrontal cortex, or PFC, is the seat of our higher brain functions, yet is extremely limited in its capacity.

- Western culture believes, incorrectly, that we have limitless free will.

- We cannot rely on it as the primary regulator of our behavior.

- Self-care, as well as meditative and mindfulness practices, significantly enhances the capability of the PFC.

NINE

# Threat vs. Intelligence

## *The Brain on Three Levels*

The human brain is an amazing organ. There's a tendency, especially with the burgeoning popular neuroscience literature, to want to neatly divide it into separate parts, each responsible for discrete functions. The reality is much more nuanced and complex. While we can identify areas and structures as being central to certain neural outcomes, the brain acts as a highly networked whole, with any given behavior being the result of multiple interactions between parts.

In order to gain a better understanding of the dynamics of the brain under stress, however, it is useful to create some rough distinctions between areas of the brain and their functions.

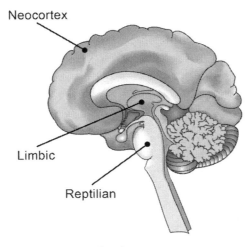

**9a-** Levels of Brain Function

An oversimplified, but useful, model for understanding the human brain examines it on three levels:[6]

- The neocortex, responsible for higher-level thinking, such as reasoning and future-oriented thinking,

- The limbic system, the emotional center of the brain, and

- The reptilian region, oriented toward base level survival.

The brain, when functioning well, processes incoming information in multiple areas of the neocortex. The limbic system accesses related memories and evaluates how an idea, decision or situation feels. We possess a complicated circuitry that assesses the relative risk and reward of any potential action and produces a "toward" or "away" motivational impulse. The reptilian system handles our autonomic functions, as well as having a special role in handling threatening situations.

Let's take a more detailed look at each level and then see how they interrelate to produce human behavior, particularly as related to threat and safety.

## Neocortex

The neocortex is the structure we tend to identify most with being human. When we view representations of the human brain, the neocortex comprises the two large folded grey lobes that dominate the picture. In common parlance, these lobes are referred to as the left and right brains. The two hemispheres are connected by the corpus callosum, which mediates the passage of information between them.

### Prefrontal Cortex

The neocortex is home to the aforementioned prefrontal cortex (PFC), the seat of conscious volition. As a reminder, the PFC is central to capacities including emotional balance, attuned communication, intuition, strategic thought, fear moderation, the ability to override impulses, empathy and morality. It is integral to volitional information processing: memorizing, recollection, and generating new insight.

## Limbic

The limbic system is shared by all mammals and is the seat of emotion and memory.

### *Resonance, Regulation and Revision*

We can describe the human limbic brain in relation to others with three processes: resonance, regulation, and revision.[7]

Limbic resonance describes how we unconsciously and continuously attune emotionally to those around us. We read facial movements and other behavior to get a feel for the internal state of the other person.

Limbic regulation refers to the ability of the emotional state of a person to implicitly affect the mood of those around him. Some people can walk into a room and their presence automatically calms. Others have the opposite effect. Interestingly, it is not necessary to have prior interaction with someone to pick up on and be quickly influenced by their state. Emotions are biologically contagious.

Limbic revision points to the capacity to rewire our own emotional circuitry through long term exposure to other individuals' emotional patterning. Surround yourself with emotionally healthy people and you, yourself, will become more emotionally stable over time. As your emotion circuits are repetitively exposed to healthy patterning, they begin to rewire in more functional configurations. Surround yourself with stressed and reactive people, especially if you have no practices to remain grounded, and you will also become more reactive.

## Imagination vs. Reality

An interesting facet of the limbic system is its inability to distinguish between imagination and reality. When we think about a situation, the emotional response in the brain is strikingly similar to that of the actual event occurring. Consider the last theatrical thriller you saw. While you knew the events to be a fictional fabrication, if the movie was good, you experienced a roller coaster of emotional suspense. Your neocortex knew it wasn't real, but the limbic system was along for the ride!

It doesn't take a movie to produce this phenomenon. Our internal thoughts constantly influence our emotional state. When we think about an event, we warm the emotional circuits associated with that situation. Compulsively replaying an experience, real or imagined, can turn those emotions into a mood. We then start to preferentially perceive the world through the lens of what is consistent with that emotional state and are unable to perceive information that disconfirms it. We may flood the brain and body with threat signals that don't, in reality, exist.

## The Value of Emotions

A legacy of the scientific revolution has been a discounting and mistrust of emotions, alongside a vaunting of the rational mind. I've had countless executive clients tell me that they'd like to "get the emotion out of their organization." I reply, without hesitation, that they would not like the result. Emotions are core to our ability to make decisions, and they are what move or motivate us to action. The word "apathy" literally means "without feelings." Absent emotion, people lose their sense of caring, motivation and ability to decide on a course of action.

Emotional states live in our bodies as well as the mind. This is how many neuroscientists believe we use our mirror neuron system to detect the emotional state of others. We model the physiology of the other person and run that information through our own somatic neural circuits. By doing so, our brains figuratively ask, "If my body were doing that, what emotion would I be having and what would it mean?"

### Emotional Literacy

As important as emotion is at a neural level, Western society is notoriously emotionally illiterate. In the past decade, one of the biggest trends in leadership development and education is teaching emotional intelligence. The emphasis on rationality and the seemingly unpredictable and destabilizing force of emotion has led us to suppress it and undervalue its role in our functioning. As such, most of us are relatively unskilled at recognizing our emotional state and unpracticed at navigating the waters of emotion in our organizations.

Wendy is fond of saying that children and animals know how you feel before you do, and there's biology to back that up. Most of the animals with which we interact lack a highly developed prefrontal cortex, as do young children. In the absence of the ability to take in information at a rational level, they rely more heavily on their ability to detect and process emotional data. It makes sense. After all, the ability to emotionally bond with a caregiver is paramount to a child's survival.

Children also lack the cognitive stories built over a lifetime that can compete or interfere with emotional recognition. Those stories help organize our perceptions, but they also get in the way of our ability to directly experience. As an example, imagine that you grew up in a family where sadness was viewed as weak. Over time, you would probably develop a way to relate to those feelings so that they wouldn't surface and cause problems. As an adult, you would likely have difficulty recognizing or gracefully responding to situations where sadness was involved. A young child, however, unpolluted by a lifetime of patterning, could sense into the emotional reality easily.

We all learn as we grow up that certain emotions are socially unacceptable depending on context. While it's useful not to inappropriately blurt out unfiltered emotions, it's not useful if those emotions are stewing in the background unrecognized, waiting to surface and cause problems. When we are unaware of our emotions and emotional patterning, we have little choice in how they play out and how they direct our lives. Leadership Embodiment practices help us develop a fine level of somatic awareness with regard to our emotional state. We can name the emotion we are experiencing and reshape our bodies to transform our emotional expression.

## Reptilian Region

The reptilian region runs in the background, producing instinctual responses and regulating autonomic body functions such as heart rate and breathing. Its functions do not require conscious thought. When was the last time you had to remember to make your heart beat? It is the most primitive area of our brain, but the most crucial to our survival. While we can withstand the compromise of other brain areas and survive, significant damage to this region generally results in death.

The reptilian system is particularly engaged in response to threat and is key to the fight, flight and freeze responses. These behaviors are crude and lack nuance, but they get the job done. You can run away; you can fight; or you can shut down. The goal is to get you out of a potentially harmful situation as efficiently as possible. Collateral damage can be dealt with once your survival has been ensured.

These reactions make sense when a tiger is chasing us or

we're under actual physical attack. They are not so useful, though, in everyday organizational settings. Stage fright is a freeze reaction, as is forgetting your point when the CEO suddenly turns her attention on you and asks a question. When somebody challenges your point in a meeting and you respond with angry defensiveness, it's a fight response. Avoiding returning a difficult call or mentally checking out during a meeting can be the psychological equivalent of flight.

## The Biology of Threat

### The Amygdalae

Within our limbic brains is a pair of structures called the amygdalae (usually referred to in the singular: amygdala). Core to arousal, they process the emotional intensity and valence of incoming stimuli, informing where we should direct our attention and which brain systems should be recruited to respond. Because of their central role in evaluating threat, the amygdalae have earned the misnomer of being the "fear center" of the brain, when in fact, this is only one facet of their function.

Stated simply, if the threat level of a given input reaches a certain threshold, these structures help determine whether your higher brain should deal with the stressor or it's best suited for a reptilian response. The higher the level of perceived threat, the more the brain defaults away from creatively responding to the present and toward habitual responses from the past or at worst, base level fight, flight and freeze.

This brain design worked well on the African Savannah, where fight, flight and freeze were usually appropriate responses to the threats humans were likely to face. That same automatic design rarely works as well in the 21st Century, where the kinds of physical threats that our evolutionary ancestors faced are relatively rare and where social threats do not result in fatal ostracism.

What the amygdala recognizes as a threat is a complicated mix of hard-wiring and references to past experiences. As humans, we instinctively know to be afraid of certain things. We see a stick in the trail and freeze, at least until such time as the brain sorts out that it's just a stick and not a snake. We saw earlier that as social animals, we also innately interpret experiences like exclusion, challenges to our status, and difference as threats.

### Amygdala Hijacks

When all of these threat indicators combine to warm the amygdalae past a certain point, these structures can divert control over our behavior from the higher brain (prefrontal cortex) to the lower, or reptilian brain. When this occurs, it is referred to as an "amygdala hijack." The amygdalae have hijacked the brain's neural resources, rerouting them to the more primitive and instinctual circuits.

Once in the grip of a hijack, we can't easily stop it. The reptilian brain is in control. It often causes us to do things we regret or are embarrassed by later. The hallmark of an amygdala hijack is that you don't experience choice about your reaction in the moment. Even as your body leaps into action, a part of you frequently recognizes that your response will cost you later. During a hijack, the neocortex is still capable of producing thoughts, but cannot generate behavior. We have the excruciatingly frustrating experience of knowing in the moment that what we're doing isn't mature or resourceful, but because the higher parts of the brain have become powerless to produce action, we do the knee jerk behavior anyway.

## Avoiding Hijacks

The trick to avoiding amygdala hijacks is two-fold. Remember, the PFC has the ability, albeit limited, to short-circuit this response cycle. By maximizing PFC functioning through healthy lifestyle, social connection, and mindfulness, we increase the threshold of threat necessary to trigger a hijack. In addition, through becoming aware of our emotional patterns and learning the early warning signals which indicate amygdala warming, we can intercept the trigger cycle before it reaches hijack levels. You want to raise the threshold for what triggers a hijack and at the same time, notice and reverse the process before it reaches that threshold.

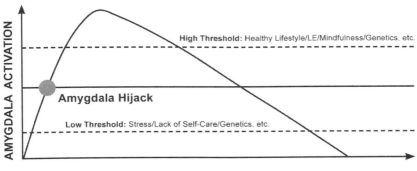

**9b-** The Amygdala Hijack

Through careful self-observation, you can train yourself to notice when an amygdala hijack is imminent. There's a period—and it's very brief—when we can recognize that we're starting to become aroused and threatened. It's a felt experience. If you catch yourself in that fleeting moment, you may be able to divert the hijack. Leadership Embodiment tools give practitioneers fine levels of somatic awareness, so that we recognize and can circumvent the threat response earlier in the cycle. Because the body reacts before the brain does consciously, if we can intercept an old behavior or perceived threat at the somatic level, we buy ourselves precious time in managing our reactions.

A key factor in determining threat is our internal evaluation of whether or not our neural system is equipped to handle the intensity of the input. Leadership Embodiment practices give us repeated somatic experience of navigating formerly overwhelming neural triggers in a more resourceful way, allowing the brain to recode previous triggers as less dangerous than they were once experienced. As we practice with Leadership Embodiment tools, we are training our nervous system that we can withstand the input.

# TEN

# Change

## *What is Change?*

I f you're reading this book, it's because you're interested in change. Change can happen at many levels. You may want to understand how to better lead your organization. You may recognize that you have personal tendencies and triggers that get in your way. You may want to relate more seamlessly and effectively with others around you. Up to this point, we've focussed on understanding where behavior comes from and the role of stress and threat in how our brains produce our actions. It's now time to look at the process of changing how we relate to ourselves and others.

## *Understanding vs. Change*

In our culture, we frequently conflate cognitive learning with motor learning. They are distinct processes, and completing one may have little relation to the other. When we learn something cognitively, the neocortex is involved in a conscious process of understanding. Through reason, we learn facts and understand the justification for a particular way of thinking or behaving.

Just understanding and buying into the rationale, however, does little to alter the patterns that drive behavior. When we cognitively vow to react to a trigger differently next time, we rarely do. The part of the brain that consciously understands the need to change and can "just say no" has extremely limited resources, and stress diminishes that capability for response inhibition even further. The pre-encoded patterns are simply too strong for the relatively weak cognitive control processes of the PFC.

In order to shift our behavior to keep pace with our cognitive understanding, we have to rehearse the new pattern so that we automatically generate the right thoughts and body responses. We do that through attention and repeated practice. Each time we notice the old impulse and activate a new response, we strengthen the motor circuitry associated with that new way of being, while allowing the old circuitry to become increasingly dormant through lack of use.

## Natural Systems and Homeostasis

All natural and relational systems exist in dynamic equilibrium. Change one part and the others must move to accommodate the shift. Systems also attempt to maintain a homeostatic balance, even if it's a dysfunctional one. Because of this, when we try to change, our first impulse is to justify reverting "just this once" to our old way of being.

The brain attempts to conserve patterns, irrespective of their usefulness in the current context. After all, our neural patterns are what have kept us alive and successfully navigating the complexities of adult life. They are what allow us to reserve our precious frontal lobes for the novel situations that necessitate their use. The brain holds onto the known preferentially over the unknown.

In addition, the people in your system know your personality and know how to trigger it. Showing up as a better and improved leader may upset the apple cart for some around you. You can expect that they may do things to trigger your personality, often not with conscious intent on their part. All of us carry internal stories that create a sense of order and predictability in our lives. When someone steps outside their defined role in our story, it can feel threatening. It forces us to change as well.

Rapid success, as good as it sounds, necessitates rapidly letting go of and/or altering old ways of being. The brain interprets the override of established neural patterns as a potential threat to our survival. In an attempt to push us back to the tried and true, the brain sends discomfort signals. The greater the magnitude or speed of the change, the greater the discomfort for all involved. This often shows up as an unidentifiable sense of unease that can only be relieved by reverting to our old way of being (or enabling someone else to assume theirs). Consciously, change sounds wonderful and refreshing. We all know, however, how easy it is to give up or to sabotage our own progress and that of those around us.

## Do Patterns Ever Go Away?

Patterns vary in their strength. Surface level habits, like the route you take to work, can be almost completely rewritten. The old way of getting to work remains somewhere in your memory banks, but it is easily replaced by a new route after sufficient repetition. Still, we've all had the experience of making a wrong turn when lost in thought and following the old route on autopilot.

The deep emotional patterns acquired in early childhood likely remain a fundamental part of our nature, even when they clearly no longer serve us. With practice over time, however, we can relate to our patterns in a substantially different way. We can learn to recognize triggers and alter our response, training our nervous system to evaluate and respond to threat more resourcefully. It's not that the pattern or impulse goes away, but that we catch ourselves before we're in its grip. We can move from trigger to awareness to Center with increasing speed and grace.

## How Neural Change Happens

### The Window of Choice

The first marker in the brain signifying that we are initiating a motor action is referred to as "readiness potential." This neural activity generally occurs approximately one half second prior to the outward manifestation of a behavior. During approximately the first 0.3 seconds, the brain readies the motor cortex to produce a behavior. Here's where the story gets curious: it's only at this point that we become consciously aware of our intent to do something.

What we experience as volitional choice may not be. Neuroscience research suggests that the unconscious brain decides on a course of action before notifying the conscious brain of its intention, not the other way around. The body is preparing for motion before the conscious brain considers whether that action is advisable.[8]

Were it not for an additional 0.2-second delay preceding the acting out of the initial impulse, free will would be nothing but a game of neural smoke and mirrors. This miniscule window is all you have to use your volitional neural capacity to decide to do something different. It's a tiny sliver of time, certainly not long enough for any deep consideration of alternatives. It's crucial to understand ahead of time how to recognize an undesirable response and have a substitute ready at hand.

We've all experienced brief moments of awareness in which we know that we should choose a new response. But then, just as quickly and despite that knowing, we choose the old familiar pathway, perhaps accompanied by a cognitive rationalization

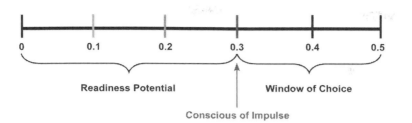

**10a** - The Window of Choice

for why it is acceptable to do so. A classic example is trying to establish healthy eating patterns. We reach for the cookie, then think "no, I shouldn't," followed by "what the heck, it's the last one and after that I won't buy any more."

When you consider overriding an established pattern, the brain produces a sense of discomfort, its way of attempting to warn you not to mess with what's worked in the past. All this in under one fifth of a second. No wonder changing habits is difficult!

### What can we do?

First, while the window to do something new is brief, so is the discomfort that drives you back to the familiar habit. And, as we will soon see, the more you make the right choice, the easier it becomes.

Second, the window of choice is too short to attempt to cognitively generate and justify a new response. Having a useful response with general application, like Centering, buys you time. If you've practiced the response, you can activate it at that crucial moment. From the open stance that Centering generates, new more resourceful neural networks will likely be available providing you with better choices.

Third, the ability to choose relies on your capacity to recognize quickly that you're headed toward an unskillful response.

The practices of paying attention to your body disposition and increasing your emotional self-literacy can have a profound impact on your ability to be at choice in your behavior. In Leadership Embodiment, the focus is first on awareness of our habitual responses as they manifest through the body. We cultivate the ability to rapidly notice when our somatic response constricts our possibilities. We bypass our cognitive stories and go straight to shifting to a more resourceful physiology.

## Repetition and Focused Attention

A part of the brain called the basal ganglia is central to encoding habits. It sits between the cognitive and motor areas of the brain, allowing it to link thought to movement. From this unique vantage point, it can translate repeated goal-directed behaviors into automated patterns. We acquire habits because they have utility in helping us navigate our lives, and we've repeated them enough times for the brain to wire them for automaticity. The cortical areas responsible for intellectual understanding may recognize that a behavioral habit has outlived its usefulness, or at a minimum needs augmentation. Conscious understanding alone, however, does nothing to decode what is hard-wired elsewhere. To do that requires consistent focused attention and practice.

U.C.L.A. neuroscientist Jeffrey Schwartz states, "…the mental act of focusing attention can hold in place brain circuits associated with what is focused on."[9] Focused practice, regularly sustained over time, leads to efficient rewiring of neural circuits. Intermittent and inconsistent practice allows the new circuits to destabilize, causing the brain to revert to the more stable, but less desirable, older circuits. While the brain is not actually a muscle, in this sense, the brain *acts* like a muscle. Sporadic vigorous workouts do very little to produce stronger muscles. Progress rapidly degrades in the off periods. Only with regular focused workouts do you see consistent results.

There is a familiar saying among neuroscientists: "Neurons that fire together, wire together." The saying, coined by neuroscientist Carla Shatz, succinctly summarizes a widely accepted theory of behavioral learning first forwarded by Canadian neuropsychologist, Donald Hebb, in 1949. You've had lots of practice firing and wiring neurons to support your old way of responding under stress. In order to stabilize a new path, the brain needs to hold its focus on a different pattern and repeat it in close proximity enough times to establish a competing pathway.

In Leadership Embodiment, the focus is on building the habit of noticing and adjusting our physiology to match our desired results. As Wendy suggests, learning the technique is only the beginning. To reap its transformational potential requires dedication and practice.

## The Role of Priming in Learning

Earlier, we briefly discussed the role of priming in directing our attention. When we think of a concept, the brain not only warms related neural circuits so that they are easily accessed, but it also preferentially directs attention to related information in the environment. Wendy calls this the Camry Effect, but we all have our personal examples. You learn a new word and suddenly see it everywhere. Your new love interest is into a band you'd never heard of, but now the name and music seem to pop up all over the place.

Our environment and thoughts continually prime our neural circuits, whether we're aware of it or not. We can make conscious use of this phenomenon by seeding our lives with objects and thoughts that prime with intentionality. When we follow the Leadership Embodiment practice of calling into mind a great and inspirational historical leader, we are priming the brain to activate the neural networks related to our associations with that person. We step out of our habitual ways of thought and allow these other networks to provide insight to the challenges that we face. The key here is to think of a figure, idea or thing that will prime your brain to access its most expansive and effective networks.

In addition, images are accompanied with an emotional connotation. When you think of a grand mountain in nature or a leader that you revere, the thought has an emotional component. From a brain perspective, emotions serve to move us into action. Feeling states are elegant shortcuts to action that bypass the thinking mind. By calling into mind an image that is accompanied by a powerful emotional state, we are not only activating the neural networks associated with that state, but we are also creating a positive disposition to action.

## Declarations and the Power of Language

Part of what makes us unique as humans is that our brains are always projecting into the future and trying to supply us with pathways to accomplish that which we wish to achieve. We are the only animal that combines this ability with language to proactively and collaboratively create futures for ourselves that differ from the here and now. Once we conceptualize a desired vision of the future, we begin to notice things in the environment that might help or hinder our achievement of that outcome.

While this phenomenon occurs largely outside of consciousness, we engage in it constantly. If I am starting a textiles company and a business reporter on the radio announces a crop failure in cotton, my ears perk up and I pay attention.

A landscape architect intent on winning a lucrative design contract might be traveling the same route and tuned into the same station, but not hear a thing. Instead, her attention might be trained on the interesting stonework on the estate she's passing.

If you pay attention, you'll become aware of your brain's constant conversation of "if this, then that." "If I finish the report before three, I'll beat traffic and run some errands close to home. If I don't finish until five, I'll stay late to avoid traffic and get caught up on my email." These kinds of mental tradeoffs are happening all the time and are driven by multiple sets of goals: get report done, avoid traffic, maximize my use of time, accomplish as many of my "to do" items as possible, etc.

Declarations are raw material that we feed into the brain's natural projection mechanisms to prime what we notice and guide our choices. When I repeat to myself, "I am committed to making a contribution," I light up the neural networks associated with contribution and commitment. My brain starts to sort for opportunities to be in service to those things that matter to me. I preferentially notice others who make contributions, big and small. I start to ask myself how I can make a positive difference in each new situation I encounter.

It's common for people to make mindless declarations that lead to less than optimal outcomes. I've often had coaching clients casually declare things like "people around here are irritating" or "I can't change." By doing so, they warm the circuits in the brain associated with irritation and inability to change. In turn, it becomes easier to notice more of what irritates them and the barriers to change that surround them. The problem is that we often carry these non-productive internal messages without ever recognizing how they shape our behavior and our perception of reality.

Strong declarations accompanied by halfhearted body postures create neural dissonance. The declaration and the body shape are incongruent. Because the neural networks associated with uncertainty, hesitancy, and lack of confidence are well-worn patterns for many of us, the priming activated by the nonverbal portion of the declaration may outweigh the verbal.

A common habit is talking about what we want to avoid rather than what we want to create. At a brain level, when we talk about what we don't want, we still prime our brains to fixate on it. With a negative command, we have not given our brain any useful priming material to orient us to notice opportunities to create what we *do* want. It's like getting in a taxi at the San Francisco airport and telling the driver that you don't want to go to Fisherman's Wharf. With the driver's only focus being avoidance of that part of the city, it's highly unlikely that you'll end up precisely where you want to be.

We all have habits of mind, mostly acquired through osmosis. Because the culture around us focuses on the negative, we are primed to do so as well. Over a lifetime, we become exceptionally good at noticing what bothers us and what we don't like, but it doesn't have to be that way. Through conscious practice, we can acquire positive habits of mind.

### The Challenge of Change

Change can be difficult and frustrating. When unwelcome change is forced upon us, it can be excrutiating. Even when we long for change, however, it can still open Pandora's Box: feelings of uncertainty, inadequacy, overwhelm, etc. When we engage in the process of change, it's useful to remind ourselves that these feelings are normal. They are simply an outgrowth of our brain's functional design which seeks to conserve patterns that have worked in the past.

We identify our personalities as ourselves. To change our personality patterns brings into question everything that we know about ourselves and how to function with others. Change at this level is the biggest challenge we can take on. When we change personality patterns, we alter the dynamic equalibrium of all our relationships. The stories we've constructed over a lifetime may no longer adequately explain what we see happening around us. We enter into a realm of "not knowing" that can feel disorienting at best and terrifying at worst.

Noticing is part of the process. Sometimes in the beginning, it can feel like you're going backwards. You've primed your brain to notice new distinctions which were formerly outside of your awareness. You now notice how your own body disposition and internal conversation may be incongurent with what you consciously espouse.

While at this initial phase, it's easy to become discouraged. Something that didn't appear to be broken before suddenly seems dysfunctional, but you've not yet gained enough skill with generating new responses to have any sense of mastery and control. It's crucial at this phase to stick with it. Remind yourself that this is a necessary and unavoidable stage in learning. Congratulate yourself for becoming a more nuanced observer of reality.

As we enter into a process of unlearning and relearning, we must be mindful to support ourselves mentally, emotionally and spiritually. Taking care of our bodies (sleep, exercise, good food, etc.), building mental and emotional fortitude through practices such as meditation, and staying connected to our communities of support will all ease the process of our evolution.

Engaging with ourselves with compassion is essential. To change and evolve our being is a heroic endeaver. It's essential to avoid the Western trap of believing that willpower and character alone will get us there and that chastizing ourselves for failure is a useful motivational technique. If you've gotten nothing else out of this section on biology, I hope it's an appreciation for the extreme limitations of our conscious rational power. Becoming angry with ourselves activates the threat mechanisms of the brain, further diminishing our capacity to learn and grow.

Instead, we need to be smart about shaping our environment to reinforce effective learning, to view the process as a journey worthy of curiousity and playful engagement, and to take on manageable levels of change. Adapting and polishing one's being is not a linear process or a one time event. Rather, it involves experimentation and discovery in interaction with others. It will necessarily include backsliding, times where the pull of the old way of being feels stronger than the new.

Remember:

**Feelings can lead you astray:** Unease, frustration, exasperation, etc. are predictable outcomes of your brain's desire to maintain the status quo.

**Backsliding is normal:** The key is to acknowledge and re-engage. As Wendy says, notice and correct as quickly as possible.

**Start small:** Don't try to do it all at once. Pick a level of change that your neurology can handle and build from there.

**Form a community:** People who know you and can support your process are invaluable.

**Be consistent:** Practice, practice, practice.

# ELEVEN

# Accelerating Evolution

The world is changing at a dizzying pace. In the early 1990s, I lived for several months in Madrid, Spain. During that time, less than twenty years ago, I relied primarily on centralized phone booths to communicate with my home base in the San Francisco Bay Area. Only the very wealthy had cell phones and even those weren't set up to handle international calling. Despite having several years of work experience and a science degree from a university considered to be a world leader in technology, the University of California at Berkeley, I didn't yet own a personal computer, nor did most of my colleagues. Email was in its infancy. In 1994, I returned to school to obtain a Masters degree from Stanford University, located in the heart of Silicon Valley. In our required research seminar, we did not cover the Internet or computer-based searches. This wasn't yet considered an accessible or reliable source of information.

Political, technological, demographic and environmental conditions are all undergoing seismic shifts. In order to remain engaged and to produce the innovative thinking required by the reality we've collectively created, we must first learn to manage ourselves. We must break free of the mindless habits of being that block resourceful engagement and learn to include, listen and speak up.

The practices of Leadership Embodiment offer a pathway for accelerating our evolution. In a culture where we primarily value data, rational thought and academic analysis, however, the methodology can seem foreign. My hope is that understanding the biology that drives our behavior may ground these practices and make them more accessible.

Most of what we do is neither conscious nor volitional. Until we become aware of what drives us, be it thoughts, emotions or body dispositions, we are powerless to change. The body takes a shape before the mind consciously identifies a thought or feeling. Our physical being is the most direct point of intervention. In the West, it is also the most ignored aspect of our emotional, intellectual and spiritual being. I hope we've intrigued you to appreciate the power of the body to change our experience. How you sit and stand will change the way you think and speak.

# REFERENCES

1.  Dana R. Carney, Amy J.C. Cuddy, and Andy J. Yap (2010). Power Posing: Brief Nonverbal Displays Affect Neuroendocrine Levels and Risk Tolerance. *Psychological Science*

2.  Naomi Eisenberger, Johanna Jarcho, Matthew Lieberman, and Bruce Naliboff (2006). An Experimental Study of Shared Sensitivity to Physical Pain and Social Rejection. *Journal of the International Association for the Study of Pain*

3.  Jamil Zaki, Jessica Schirmer, and Jason Mitchell (2011). Following the Crowd: Brain Images Offer Clues to How and Why We Conform. *Psychological Science*

4.  Anita Williams Woolley, Christopher F. Chabris, Alexander Pentland, Nada Hashmi, and Thomas W. Malone (2010). Evidence for a Collective Intelligence Factor in the Performance of Human Groups. *Science Express*

5.  Daniel J. Siegel (2007). The Mindful Brain, *W. W. Norton & Company, Inc.*

6.  Derived from the triune brain model first introduced by Paul MacLean in the 1960s.

7.  Thomas Lewis, Fari Amini, Richard Lannon (2000). A General Theory of Love. *Random House*

8.  Benjamin Libet, Curtis A. Gleason, Elwood W. Wright, and Dennis K. Pearl (1983). Time of Conscious Intention to Act in Relation to Onset of Cerebral Activity (Readiness Potential): The Unconscious Initiation of a Freely Voluntary Act. *Brain, A Journal of Neurology*

9.  Donald D. Price, G. Nicholas Verne and Jeffrey M. Schwartz (2006). Plasticity in Brain Processing and Modulation of Pain. *Progress in Brain Research, Vol. 157*

# ACKNOWLEDGMENTS
## Wendy Palmer

Many people have knowingly and unknowingly contributed to the ongoing development and refinement of the Leadership Embodiment concepts, techniques, and practices presented in this book. I am deeply grateful to the all of the clients and students whose questions and insights have, over the years, helped the work grow and evolve. The people who have been touched by Leadership Embodiment continue to inspire and encourage me to persist in bringing Leader Embodiment out into the world.

Giving life to a book and delivering it into the hands of readers takes a group of committed individuals. This book is the result of much time, effort, and dedication of a number of people. I would like to give a special thanks to the people below, who have directly influenced the manifestation of this book.

For quite some time, I had looked to explore the LE perspective with someone who had both scientific knowledge and an interest in leadership. When Janet Crawford agreed to collaborate with me, I was delighted—working with and learning from Janet has been a wonderful experience as the process of bringing book to life has unfolded. It was auspicious that Joan Marie Passalacqua, a long time friend and student of the work was able to commit to being editor and thinking partner. Her editing of *The Intuitive Body* many years ago helped me transform my manuscript from hesitant beginnings into a clear, precise form. It has been a pleasure to get to know our illustrator, Jen Mahoney—her ability to adapt to our needs is as inspiring as her gift as an artist. To John Lund, our fabulous photographer and creator of the cover art, thank you for your generosity and support. Many thanks to Colleen Dwire, our talented book designer, who shepherded our project through the production process.

Deep thanks to Gordon Johnson who offered me a much needed place to write in solitude—the beauty and quietude of Bermuda allowed me to gain momentum with the manuscript—upon my return I was able to keep it moving forward. To my daughter and partner, Tiphani, thank you for all your love and support during this process.

Big thanks to Jackie McGrath for her continued support and many opportunities to work with powerful and interesting people—many of whom inspired the expansion of my conscious embodiment work into *Leadership Embodiment* to specifically address the challenges of leadership.

Thank you to Karen White for your friendship, support, and our numerous discussions about leadership and language. Thanks to Linda Bush for donating time and insightful copy editing. Special thanks to Michele Seymour and Judy Torrison for their eleventh-hour "cold reads" of Part One.

To the community in the EU/UK, Amanda Ridings, Matthew Dodwell, Anouk Brack, John Tuite, James Knight, Michele Seymour, Beth Follini, Pierre Goirand and Paul King—thank you for your continued support, inspiration, and friendship.

# ACKNOWLEDGMENTS
## Janet Crawford

While few of us continue to live as our ancestors did on the African Savannah, we still owe our survival and our triumphs to a web of human relationships, both chosen and accidental.

I was deeply honored to be invited by Wendy Palmer to collaborate in the writing of this book. Wendy is a pioneer whose ideas are transformational, and it's been a delight and pleasure to work with her.

Thank you to:

My clients, who open their lives to me and give me rich territory in which to explore applications of neuroscience and human biology to the world of business.

The inspiring group of colleagues with whom I test my thinking: Wendy Appel, Susan Bethanis, Karen Lam, Karen Seidman, Alyssa Levy, Shoshana Rosenfeld, Ade Mabogunje, Victor Hwang, Greg Horowitt, Miguel Franco, Thuy Sindell, Dave Ancel, Ann Badillo, Christine Cavanaugh, Regan Bach, Kay Sandberg, Reza Ahmadi, Bill McLawhon, Stephanie Barbour, Amanda Blake, and so many others. Special gratitude to my compatriots in the conCenter Alliance: Lisa Marshall, Larry Solow, Dee Kinder, Karen Bading and Charles Feltman.

My teachers: Lucy Freedman and the Syntax Communication Modeling Corporation, Peter Kline, Michael Grinder, Julio Olalla and the Newfield Network, and the new wave of neuroscientists who investigate the social brain. You inspire me.

The talented team who brought this book from raw text into a finished product: Joan Marie Passalacqua,

Jennifer Mahoney, Richard Leeds, Linda Bush, John Lund and Colleen Dwire.

I've been blessed with a family and set of intimate friends who love and support me unconditionally. Deep gratitude to:

My dear friends Dana Smith, Jamy Madeja, Julia Logan, Janice Lum, Mary Hinman and Don Baker, who keep me sane and remind me what's important,

Lisa Marshall, who is a thought partner of unparalleled insight and the best friend anyone could hope for,

John Popplewell, who tells me I have something big to contribute to the world when my belief wavers and patiently puts up with me when writing makes me grumpy,

My family, Steve, Robin and Audrey Crawford, whose love, humor, intelligence and kindness sustain me; and my parents, Jack and Frances Crawford, who gave me a lusty intellectual curiosity, but whose true gift was instilling in me the importance of contribution and of living a principled and meaningful life.

48665682R00114

Made in the USA
Lexington, KY
09 January 2016